Praise for *I Remember When*

"This book makes a major contribution toward helping people use the reminiscence process. The ideas are innovative and provide new approaches to a popular activity. The multisensory approach to reminiscing is particularly innovative and exciting. It allows the reader to adapt the reminiscing process for those who may be disabled or who may have dementia. This book is a must for those who work with older people."

Dr. Barbara Haight, R.N.C., Ph.D. Professor of Gerontological Nursing, Medical University of South Carolina, Charleston, SC

"A veritable reminiscence encyclopedia! This book incorporates in one volume research resources and "how-to's" for a broad range of reminiscence and storysharing opportunities. Such a single volume would have been a great help to me in training reminiscence volunteer visitors during my years at AARP."

Betty Davis, Former AARP Reminiscence Program Coordinator

"Reminiscence therapy is used by a variety of disciplines, and this how-to manual should be helpful to all. An especially important focus on the senses is particularly helpful in group work with frail elders. Another section describes an exercise called "bring-a-thing." Both of these exercises are excellent for caregivers to use with persons suffering from dementia, especially Alzheimer's disease. For neophytes wanting to begin reminiscence therapy, either with relatives or in their profession, I highly recommend this manual as a resource."

Irene Burnside, R. N., Ph.D. Professor Emerita, San Jose State University, CA

"Thorsheim and Roberts provide an exceptional resource that deftly blends theory and practice. Particularly helpful are the numerous, easy-to-use conversation starters applicable to various clinical settings. This resource will quickly become worn by practitioners who value the integrative and enjoyable process of reminiscing."

Mark Holman, Director of Network Development, Lutheran Services in America (LSA)

"I Remember When offers a complete introduction to the remarkable life affirming power of reminiscence and storytelling. The book is a practical invitation for story tellers and listeners alike."

Bill Webb, MT-BC, University Good Samaritan Society, Minneapolis, MN

"I Remember When *is a very valuable reminiscence resource guide aimed at a diverse audience ranging from active seniors ready to write life stories on the Internet to those facilitating storytelling by nursing home residents. The book includes many innovative suggestions for reminiscence activities including pump-primers based on the five senses, bring-a-thing parties, and conversation links (a website created by the authors for exchanging life stories)."*

Ellen Bouchard Ryan, Ph.D.
Professor of Gerontology, McMaster University, Hamilton Ontario.

"Drs. Thorsheim and Roberts provide well researched and thought-provoking activities on the use of Reminiscence and Life Review. Their insight and sensitivity will undoubtedly improve the quality of life for older adults."

Sandy Manderfeld, Director, Reminiscing Program, Senior Helping Hands, St. Cloud Hospital, MN

"This book is a helpful guide to older adult activities in the congregation and community. It is also a good training tool in varied settings."

Dorothy Stein, Director of Gerontological Ministries, Emerita, Evangelical Lutheran Church in America

I Remember When

Activity Ideas to Help People Reminisce

by

Howard Thorsheim, Ph.D., and Bruce Roberts, Ph.D.

Library of Congress Cataloging in Publication Data
Main Entry under Title:
I Remember When
Activity Ideas to Help People Reminisce
1. Reminiscence 2. Storytelling 3. Activities 4. Elders

ISBN 0-943873-17-7
LCCN 99-072912

Cover and Book Design: Bonnie Fisk-Hayden
Front cover photo © 1999 *STAR TRIBUNE*/Minneapolis-St. Paul

Elder Books
PO Box 490 Forest Knolls CA 94933
PH: 1 800 909 COPE or 415 488 9002
Email: Info@ElderBooks.com

TABLE OF CONTENTS

Photographs and Illustrations

LIST OF FIGURES

ACKNOWLEDGMENTS

The sure-fire group activities in this book are research based and field tested and have been developed with partial support from the Fulbright Commission, the Norway-Marshall Fund, the American-Scandinavian Foundation, the National Institute on Drug Abuse, the Blandin Foundation, and St. Olaf College, to whom we wish to express our thanks. We acknowledge, with great appreciation, the special help of colleagues at the Norwegian Gerontological Institute in Oslo, Norway; the Portland Age-Wise Senior Community Video Project of Portland State University; the University of Oslo Institute of Psychology; the University of Bergen Institute of Psychology; the University of Bergen Division for Geriatric Medicine; the Diakonhjemmet Sykehus in Oslo; the Diakonhjemmet Sosialhøgskole in Oslo; the University of Wales at Cardiff; and the Ullevål Center for Social Networks and Health of the Norwegian Social Department, Oslo. We thank our co-participants in the December 1988 Fulbright Colloquium at the University of Wales (Newton, Wales) Conference entitled "Communication, Health, and the Elderly" for their encouragement to continue working to develop this book.

We would like to thank specific individuals for their help and their ideas conveyed through meetings, conversations, and/or their writings that have influenced our work: Jakob Aano; Rune Aarseth; Leona Abel; Mara Adelman; Sharon Roe Anderson; Berit Ås; Arthur Baagason; Marian Baagason; Charles Balcer; Bela Banathy; Michael Basseches; James Beddow; Noreen Benson; Kirsten Benum; Eva Beverfelt; Jan Bjørnsen; Lois Burgoyne; Robert Butler; Marvis Canon; William Cayley; Andrea Christianson; Leona Collins; Dick and Anne Conner; Nikolas Coupland; Carol Lynn Courtney; Svein Olav Daatland; Liv Dahl; Odd Stefan Dalgard; Arild Daleng; Kirsten Danielsen; Betty Davis; Bothild Deichman-Sørensen; Elsa Døhlie; Halvard Dyb; Frøydis Lohne Enes; Judy Enestvedt; Richard Evenson; Mary Field; Alene Fink; Arnstein Finset; Mary Anne Fitzpatrick; Gudbrand Fossan; Live Fyrand; Ragnhild Galtung; Heidi Gautun; Howard Giles; Geir Gundersen; Odd Gundtvedt; Eva Hagen; Gunhild Hagestad; Barbara Haight; Karen Hansen; Berger Hareide; Kenneth Heap; Anne Helseth; Peter Hjort; Maryjude Hoeffel; George Holt; Tordis Høgeid; Ida Hydle; Reidun Ingebretsen; Robert Jacobsen; Anne Jebens; Susan Keljo; Jim Kelly; Gwen Kenney; Robert Kleiner;

Sonya Knutsen; Helge Kvanvig; Robert Kleiner; Ronald Klug; Orlyn Kringstad; Knut Laake; Marit Lauvli; David and Ruth Legvold; Martin Leine; Ivar Lie; Susan Lingsom; Åsmund Lunde; Kolbein Lyng; David Maitland; Fernanda Malmin; Ken Maton; Anne McCracken; Toni McNaron; Chandra Mehrotra; Lars Mikkelsen; Tammy Nolan; Randi Nord; Phillip Norum; Aase-Marit Nygård; Margaret Hayford O'Leary; Bjørn Olsen; James K. Olson; Reidar Ommundsen; Omar Otterness; Allan Øvereng; Guido Peeters; Miriam Peifer; Novella Perrin; Dorothy Peters; Fins Petersen; Sandra Manderfeld; Ann McCracken; Meg Pick; Lois and Sidney Rand; Julian Rappaport; Emelda Rasmussen; Tracy Revenson; Suzanne Riesman; Jan Roberts; Karen Rook; Lee Rowe; Marie-Berg Rusten; Ellen Bouchard Ryan; Otto Christian Rø; Ragnhild Hovengen Sætre; Jorunn Otterlei Sand; Seymour Sarason; Per Saugstad; Åge Seiersten; Sol Seim; Lisbeth Skjeggerud; Dorothy Skårdal; Olaf Skårdal; Britt Slagsvold; Per Erik Solem; Jane Soli; Elisabet Sommerfeldt; Einar Strand; Ivar Stugu; Beth Gettys Sturkey; Per Sundby; Brian Sundermeier; Magna Svanevik; Kirsten Thorsen; Gladys Thorsheim; Julie Loken Thorsheim; Mary Thorsheim; Mary Titus; Mette Uthus; Toril Utne; Ola Valland; Martha Vargas; Susan Warner; Elaine Westerdahl-Delaney; Per Wiedswang; John M. Wiemann; Laird Yock.

We would like to thank Gordeen Gorder for her valuable editing expertise during the preparation of this book.

DEDICATION

We dedicate this book to Robert Butler who, through his research and encouragement of the practice of Life Review, has pioneered work in reminiscing and telling life stories as a way to empower people. Dr. Butler dedicated his professional life to promoting the dignity of elders.

Howard Thorsheim, Robert Butler, and Bruce Roberts

~ Chapter 1 ~

Why Reminiscing is Important

REMEMBER BACK TO A TIME WHEN

- Someone asked you what was on your mind or in your heart and shared the same kinds of things with you
- Someone took time to listen to you and appreciated what you said
- Someone invited you to become involved in an activity, or
- Someone asked for your help.

IT FEELS GOOD WHEN PEOPLE LISTEN TO US, express their appreciation of us, are open with us, and include us. When this happens, we have a sense of well-being and a feeling that our life has meaning. When we are asked to tell stories of our life experiences and someone listens to us, we feel empowered.

DEFINITION OF EMPOWERMENT: To feel empowered is to have a sense of well-being and a sense that your life has important meaning. You have a good sense of identity and some control over things that really matter to you personally. You care about others and feel that you belong and are accepted, that you are asked to help in important ways, and that you are appreciated for who you are and what you can do.

In contrast to the times when you have enjoyed being listened to, remember back to a time in your own experience when
- No one asked you about what was on your mind or in your heart,
- No one took time to listen to you, and you felt alone,
- No one encouraged you to join in an activity, or
- No one asked you for help.

It does not feel good when no one listens to us. We feel alone; we feel excluded from what others are thinking or doing. When no one asks us to help, we do not feel appreciated. This can be discouraging, to say the least. When we do not have an opportunity to speak of the meaningful aspects of our lives, we feel disempowered.

DEFINITION OF DISEMPOWERMENT: To feel disempowered is to feel insignificant, with a sense that your life has little meaning. You feel a lack of control over things that really matter to you personally. You feel like an outsider who is not included or asked to help. You feel that people do not appreciate you as much as you would like.

An antidote to disempowerment is to find and express our own voices, to tell our own stories, and to listen as others do the same. It is then that we discover aspects we have in common. The stories are the connecting links with our friends, relatives, neighbors, co-workers, and others in our community, wherever that community may be.

Telling stories of experiences and listening to others is as natural as breathing. Still there are many barriers that make getting to know and care about others a difficult task. One of the most common barriers to reminiscing is a lack of skills or practice in telling our own stories and in listening to others tell theirs.

This book is written to help you and others share life stories about common interests and life experiences. People of all ages like to talk about themselves and to be listened to. Talking about stories of life experiences empowers people, whatever their age.

It is important to remember that reminiscing also includes talking about events and objects that are recent. Reminiscing does not always have to center on the distant past.

RESEARCH IDENTIFIES NEED FOR REMINISCING ACTIVITIES

AS RESEARCHERS WE ARE INTERESTED IN THE VALUE of storytelling within our society. A federal research grant enabled us to acquire the scientific data that established the need for social support activities such as reminiscing. Our research involved about ten thousand people in twenty-four communities. Important aspects of the research findings are briefly discussed here.[1]

First, the research showed that opportunities for social support from family and friends are fewer as we grow older. There are many reasons for the reduced support, such as having moved away from family and friends because of career opportunities, experiencing health problems, and needing to live in particular climates.

Second, as we grow older, opportunities for receiving esteem from family and friends are fewer. We receive esteem when someone lets us know that they appreciate us for some quality or competency we have. Our research shows the drop in esteem to be particularly dramatic for men at age sixty-five, at the time of retirement. Esteem received from others drops to near zero. New stress on marital relationships sometimes occurs when men are around the house most of the time. Men who were formerly at work are now looking for meaningful ways to be engaged. One woman told us how her husband's retirement led him to take control of the household in ways that annoyed her. "He even alphabetized my spices, and now I can't find what I need when I need it," she reported.

Third, our research shows that opportunities to talk about our interests drop as we grow older. Because our interests reflect what we find meaningful in life, this loss of opportunities can be devastating.

Our research also demonstrates that people who remain active as they grow older do not lose social support, expressions of esteem from others, or opportunities to talk with others about life experi-

---

[1] See Chapter 11 for more information about the research.

ences. Active people have the skills to learn other people's names, care about others, and ask other people to become engaged. They know how to link up with others so they find opportunities to reminisce, listening to one another's stories of life experiences, from earlier days and current times. People who maintain social contacts feel a sense of belonging.

This information prompted us to research if there are any health benefits from reminiscing. We decided to study what happens to people's blood pressure and heart rate during a storytelling/listening activity. In a preliminary study, we found evidence that strongly suggested that systolic blood pressure and heart rate are lowered significantly below resting baseline levels when people listen to meaningful reminiscing. In contrast, when people listen to stories or to information that is not meaningful, there is no similar lowering of blood pressure and heart rate.

We view our findings about the benefits for blood pressure and heart rate to be preliminary results that need to be examined in future studies. We are conservative about claims based on this pilot study.

This book provides storytelling activities that bring back opportunities for talking about interests and for developing a network of social support that will provide a source of esteem from others. Research suggests that the benefits of story-sharing include a renewed sense of well-being and happiness, and perhaps even better psychological and physical health.

Members of the Breakfast Group share coffee and stories:
Ansgar Sovik, Daniel Palm, Albert Finholt, Bill Narum, and Tom Porter
(Photo by Erika Nelson © 1993 *St. Olaf Magazine*, St. Olaf College)

We know a group of retired men and women who have been conversing informally about their life stories for many years. They meet once a week and call themselves the Breakfast Group. From time to time, they have taken turns reflecting on a topic of interest to them, such as "How My Political Views Have Evolved."

Another topic they discussed in the early days of their group was "Decisions I Have Made." Their reflections led many to discover that what they originally regarded as decisions they controlled were often influenced in major ways by external events. Their changing perspectives are a good example of what David Maitland in his book, *Aging as Counterculture* (New York: Pilgrim Press, 1991), calls "a growing appreciation for how much like others one is and, on the other hand, an increasing awareness of the influence of external events on one's life."

The long-term success of the Breakfast Group attests to its benefit for these people. They've gained a sense of fellowship. They all have a chance to contribute to each other in some way. And they reflect on their own life experiences in a positive light.

Talking about stories of life experiences empowers people, whatever their age. So take a look at the basic skills for encouraging reminiscing presented in the next section. You may be surprised at how familiar they are to you.

THREE SKILLS FOR ENCOURAGING REMINISCING

THERE ARE SOME BASIC SKILLS that help build self-esteem and a sense of identity. They are skills you already have. You can use them today. They are

- Helping people talk
- Helping people actively listen
- Helping people gain a sense of trust

You have done each of these things all of your life. A secret in encouraging good reminiscing is to use all three of these skills more-or-less at the same time. Let's take a look at each of these skills and then examine briefly how they fit together.

Skill #1—Helping People Talk

Helping people talk about what is meaningful to them affirms them and their life experiences. Sometimes you only have to ask a person to tell you about an interesting life experience. But for many people, such a question is

Talking, listening, building a sense of trust

too broad, so they may respond with something like, "Oh, I can't think of anything right now." If you get this kind of response, you may want to use another approach.

One strategy is to ask the person about something specific. For instance, you can say, "I'd be very interested in hearing what happened to you the day the new school opened." Then the person is reminded of a very specific event. Furthermore, and perhaps most importantly, the person also knows this is an experience that you want to hear about. But what if you don't know enough about what is meaningful in the person's life to ask such a specific question? What clues might help you discover what is important to them?

It's easy. Simply look around for things that the person has collected, like a knickknack put on a shelf or something the person is wearing. You have probably used this skill lots of times. Generally speaking, you can assume that the things you see—a picture, an artifact, or a special piece of jewelry—has meaning to this person. You may say something like, "Mary, this is a pretty picture. Would you be willing to tell me more about it?" This approach can work like a charm.

We have developed this idea into an activity called *Bring-a-Thing* through extensive field testing in America and Europe. The *Bring-a-Thing* activity is mentioned throughout the book and the steps involved in leading the activity are provided in Chapter 7.

Skill #2—Helping People Listen Actively

We have heard people say, "Well, of course I can listen. I have two ears, don't I?" But most of us can recall a time we have tried to talk to another person, but that person looked around the room instead of at us, acted as if we weren't talking, or interrupted with another story. We don't feel very good when this happens.

The lack of active listening skills is important for several reasons. First, if you are the talker, it is disempowering to you when your partner does not listen well. Second, a person who does not listen well misses opportunities to connect his own life to what the talker is saying. Third, when people don't listen to the stories they tell each other, good opportunities to form friendships and a sense of community are lost.

We like the expression *respectful listening.* When you listen actively, you are conveying a sense of respect for the talker and for the experiences being described. Respectful listening shows that the listener is interested in what is said. We build a sense of common ground, friendship, and community when we listen with respect.

Aspects of respectful listening include the following skills:
- **Developing good eye contact.** Look at the speaker when he or she is sharing a life experience.
- **Asking open questions** such as "Could you say more about that?" When we ask for more details, the speaker is usually pleased. For example, if the speaker tells of a special day or event, it is helpful to ask who else might have been there, what happened, what the weather was like, or what the surroundings looked like on that particular day.
- **Paraphrasing what the speaker is saying** in your own words. Give a very quick summary of what the speaker just told you by saying something like "So after you visited your cousin, you took up horseback riding!"
- **Reflecting on the feelings** being expressed in the speaker's story. You may say things like "It sounds like you had a happy time."

- **Giving the speaker "air time"** by not interrupting. Don't start telling your own story until the speaker has finished. This may be harder than you think, for their story may remind you of a wonderful experience you want to share.
- **Respecting the speaker's experiences.** Don't belittle what the speaker did just because you would have done it differently.
- **Concentrating on what the speaker is saying.** If you are going to find some common ground with the speaker, you will need to think about what is being said. If necessary, ask questions that would make the story more interesting, but don't let your mind wander.

Skill #3—Helping People Gain a Sense of Trust

Sometimes you may be reluctant to tell about the really important experiences in your life because you are not sure what the listener will do with what is said. You may wonder if the listener will care about what you say, make fun of your ideas, or tell others about your story without your permission. When you have a trusting relationship with others, you know that what you say will be treated with respect.

When you reminisce with people you do not know well, such as a co-worker or someone you are visiting, you will not have already established a trusting relationship. Think about how much you want to reveal beforehand so you will not inadvertently talk about more than you feel comfortable discussing.

It is sometimes helpful to have a clear idea of what you are going to talk about. When speakers and listeners both know what is going to happen next, they are more likely to feel comfortable and are better able to communicate a sense of respect and dignity as they share their life experiences. Sometimes, in more free-wheeling and sponta-neous groups where people do not know each other well and do not know what will happen next, they can feel out of control.

When you begin a conversation with somebody you do not know well, it is important not to probe too deeply at first. Make sure the talker feels comfortable with what he or she is saying. One good way to start a conversation is to focus on an artifact, picture, or other object that the person has on public display. These things can feel safe for the person because they provide a boundary for the story being told. The object connects the speaker to relationships and experiences.

PUTTING THESE THREE SKILLS TOGETHER

SO THERE YOU HAVE IT—THE THREE SKILLS of good reminiscing: (1) helping people talk about what is meaningful to them; (2) helping people (including yourself!) listen with respect; and (3) helping people develop a sense of trust in the reminiscing relationship.

These three skills often work naturally together. Good listening skills include skills that help people talk about what is meaningful to them. By looking for meaningful things to talk about, you will signify an interest in an experience that is important to the person. You will also help define some important boundaries for your conversation.

For Better or For Worse®   **by Lynn Johnston**

Stories are all around us

(© Lynn Johnston Productions Inc. /Dist. by United Feature Syndicate, Inc.)

Stories are all around us. All one needs to do is use these three skills to spark the stories. Much of the rest of this book helps you discover ways in which you can use the three skills together in a variety of places.

BENEFITS OF THIS BOOK FOR YOU

CONVERSATION IS A NATURAL ACTIVITY. As people converse about their life experiences, they have an opportunity to maintain and build their networks of mutual social support that are vital to their health.

People who experience the meaningfulness of reminiscing may, in turn, begin to share their stories with other people. You will then have helped increase the quality of their community life!

As you actively partici-pate in reminiscing, you may be surprised that you too are benefiting from this activity. In *Aging as Counterculture: A Vocation for the Later Years,* David Maitland notes that by pay-ing attention to our accumulated experiences, we are more likely to see those previous experiences in a new and beneficial

Gerald Bloedow and Margaret Pederson sharing their stories

light. By sharing stories from your own life, you may discover seg-ments of your own experiences in other people's stories and you may increase your own sense of well-being. In addition, the enjoyable sto-ries you hear and share can provide the grist for further conversations with other people in your life.

We have asked many people why reminiscing is important. Following are some of their helpful comments. As you read of these real-life benefits, think of them as potential benefits for you too, not just for the people you are conversing with.

- "When people begin telling their stories, sometimes called small talk, that's when friendship begins."
- "Telling life experiences enriches the group as people come to know one another."
- "Shared life experiences helped me realize I was not alone in what I have experienced. There is a gift in that. It is empow-ering."
- "Stories helped me make connections. They are like bridges."
- "Stories of life experiences link what's meaningful to us."

- "Stories evolve. I tell a bit, and then tell more. A story has a life of its own."
- "Telling about life experiences helps us break silences in our society and in our lives."
- "Stories that others tell renew me; they help me discover new things. It is like listening to myself."
- "A group may disempower an individual if it prevents that person from telling his or her story."

Stories start with the speaker; but as the stories progress, listeners become involved. This telling and listening—the two-way street of sharing life experiences—empowers everyone in the group. The benefits of storysharing may be summarized as follows:

- People feel connected and less alone in their experiences. They develop friendships.
- They feel more respected. They see themselves as unique and they realize they have something to contribute.
- Surprisingly, people develop more trust in others and in themselves as well.
- Important insights are gained from each other.

The conversation activities in this book can make your work and your visits with people easier, more fun, and more effective. These hands-on, failure-free tools will be useful and enjoyable for you, whether you are a healthcare professional who works with retired men and women or a friend or relative who visits someone. The reminiscing tools we discuss are based on our extensive research and experience. We know with certainty that you can put these tools to use immediately.

~ Chapter 2 ~

Reminiscing Activities
You Can Do Right Now

LET'S BEGIN WITH A SIMPLE WAY for you to reminisce by yourself. You have probably done something like this countless times. The tips offered here should remind you how easy it is to reminisce.

Once you've seen how enjoyable it is to reminisce by yourself, you will want to share this activity with others. We suggest a straightforward way to try out reminiscing one-on-one as you visit and work with people. We provide a host of tips about possible pump-primers or memory joggers that work well. We then suggest a number of ways to spread reminiscing around to help people link with each other. It is important to reminisce in a way that feels comfortable to you. Give it a try!

REMINISCING BY YOURSELF

Sell yourself on the idea of reminiscing by doing it yourself. Your own experiences will help you when you encourage others to reminisce.

Look around and find an object you have saved. It may be a picture on the wall or something you have set on a shelf. It may be a memento of an experience or something you are wearing, like a ring or a scarf.

Memories sparked by a picture on the wall

Let's pretend you have focused on a picture on the wall. Sit back, take a deep breath, and reflect for a few moments. Think of a story that goes with the picture. Where did the picture come from? What experience does it remind you of? Is there a special person or relationship that you think about when you look at it? Perhaps there is a special event that comes to mind as you look at the picture. What feelings come to mind? Allow yourself time to enjoy your reflections.

If you don't have an object to look at right now, think about something back at your house, apartment, or workplace. Bring to mind a memento, vacation photo from the lake, stuffed animal, coffee mug, or lamp. While you have that object in your mind's eye, think about those associated memories just as you would if the memento were right in front of you.

A vacation photo stirs memories

As you think about the experiences associated with the object in front of you or in your mind's eye, you are reminiscing. The people and events you are thinking about are a story. In this case, you are telling the story to yourself. Notice how good the story makes you feel. That feeling is similar to how other people will feel when you help them to reminisce.

Here is an example of Howard's reminiscing by himself as he looked at a recent picture taken while he was waxing his family's Model A Ford.

"When I was in high school my sister Mary and I pooled our money and bought a 1930 Model A Ford. One night I took the car to a football game with a group of friends. After the game, my friends and I went back to the car to go home—but the car would not start.

I tried everything I could think of to get it going, but the engine would not start. I suggested that my friends get out and push and I would try to start the car by engaging the clutch when we got rolling fast enough.

Howard Thorsheim waxing the family's Model A Ford

My friends pushed me about three blocks. By then they were huffing and puffing; but in their high-school exuberance, they thought it was great fun to be pushing the Model A.

At that point I remembered there was a gas shutoff lever under the dashboard. I had been taught to always shut off the gas lever when leaving the car so no one else could start the car. I looked down and sure enough—I had shut the lever off before the game.

As I reached down to turn on the switch so the starved engine would have fuel, one of my friends who was pushing on the right side saw me. "What are you doing?" he asked. "Is that a gas shut off valve that you are turning back on? Have we been pushing a car with the gas shut off all this time?"

I had to admit that yes, indeed, that is what had happened. Well, you can imagine the razzing I got for trying to start the car and asking my friends to push it when I had shut the gas off.

That experience happened about forty years ago, and our family still has that Model A Ford. The car provides many opportunities to tell the story about the day I asked my friends to push me when I had forgotten to turn on the gas valve!"

Notice how Howard's object—his Model A Ford—served as a stimulus for him to tell about his experience with high school friends, in addition to telling about the old car.

REMINISCING ONE-ON-ONE AS YOU VISIT AND WORK

CONVERSATION ONE-ON-ONE IS THE WAY most of us reminisce with others. You can find opportunities for reminiscing popping up when visiting with people, taking a break during work, or stopping by to greet somebody. Even brief verbal exchanges can pick up on topics of mutual interest. Here's a story told to us by a friend about a conversation he once had on an elevator.

"Kara and I both arrived at the elevator at the same time. She was carrying a potted plant, an African violet. I asked her, 'Who are you going to give the plant to?'

'Well,' she smiled and said, 'this is mine. It was just given to me by my co-workers in celebration of my birthday. They know I like plants!'

Kara's African violet

When the elevator arrived, we got on and pushed the buttons for our floors. After I wished her happy birthday, I asked where she was born, and she said, 'Newark, New Jersey.' Since we were working in Chicago at the time, I found that interesting. I was from the Garden State too. I was ready to ask her how she got from New Jersey to Illinois when the elevator got to my floor and I had to get out. I look forward to the next time our paths cross so we can pick up the conversation where it left off."

Note how a brief conversation led to the discovery of a common experience and created an eagerness for the storyteller to meet with Kara in the future.

We encourage you to try out reminiscing right now. Seek out somebody around you, even if you only have a few minutes.

If we were to point out a secret to good reminiscing experiences, it would be the importance of identifying an object that is likely to have meaning for the person you are speaking with. You can initiate a conversation by referring to the object. Then use good talking, listening, and trusting skills. As you walk up to a person, comment briefly about something you notice. The person may then begin to tell you more about the object. Then ask follow-up questions to show your interest in what the person is telling you.

Several people share their stories

Always remember to show your respect by being sensitive to the information you are being told. If you sense that someone is telling you a story that is of a sensitive nature, or perhaps may be confidential, it is very important to check with the teller to see if he or she wants you to hold that story in confidence. We all appreciate knowing our stories will not be repeated if we don't want them to be, so attention to confidentiality is important.

~ Chapter 3 ~

Priming the Pump, Using Our Senses

PRIMING THE PUMP was an important step in the days when water came from a well and was drawn up manually by a pump. Bruce was raised in the city, but worked as a cowboy on the large Bug Ranch in Wyoming during summers in the early '50s. This story is about Bruce's first encounter with priming the pump.

Priming a pump like the one in Bruce's story

"One bright, hot June day during the month-long calf roundup, we stopped by a graying old log house in the middle of the sagebrush country, a short distance from Powder River. The cowboys referred to this long-vacant ranch as 'The Love Place' after a Mr. Love who homesteaded there years ago. Since we had a few minutes while waiting for others to catch up with us, we poked around inside.

The floor was covered with about two inches of light-colored dirt. There was hardly a stick of furniture left in the four rooms. But alongside the small sink in the tiny kitchen was a worn-out, old water pump. I grabbed the handle and gave it a few pumps. 'Well's dry,' I pronounced. 'Nothing in there to come out.'

One of the cowboys looked at me with curiosity. 'Haven't you ever heard about priming the pump?' I didn't say anything because I didn't want to appear stupid, but I hadn't the slightest idea what he meant. Somebody handed me a can of water and told me to pour it very slowly down the inside of the pump while pumping the handle. I did as I was told, not really knowing what to expect. Soon the handle got harder to pump. There seemed to be more friction against the side of the pipe going down into the well as the old flange began to swell up from the water I was adding. When I pushed the pump handle down, the connections began to seal and create a vacuum. The water deep inside the well was drawn to the surface, and soon cool water was flowing into the sink—and also onto the floor because there was no drain left in the sink.

The cowboys gathered around and enjoyed the cool water while I continued to pump the handle. I felt victorious, but I wasn't exactly sure what I had done. The cowboys told me that the water I added was called a pump-primer. It served to draw out the water that had been in the pipes all along."

Memories are often like that. They are down there, waiting to refresh us. Yet without some kind of pump-primer, our well of memories may seem dry. We may feel we have nothing to talk about. Mementos, however, can be like the can of water we added to the pump. Mementos can draw those experiences to the surface, where they can be heard and enjoyed by others. Mementos can be used as pump-primers. They are saved because they connect the owner with meaningful experiences and relationships; they help people tell their stories about everyday experiences. They help speakers and listeners connect. When people share stories back and forth, they not only have an enjoyable conversation, but they understand each other better. They build friendships.

Many objects are pump-primers for conversations because they trigger memories by stimulating our senses of sight, touch, smell, or hearing. For example, think how a song can trigger memories of something associated with the era when that song was popular. The smell of an old friend's perfume, the feel of sand, or the sounds of Christmas carols may stimulate memories of friends, places, or activities of long ago.

Our senses provide a window to our memories.

SIGHT

WHILE MANY OF THE ACTIVITIES we have described use objects as stimuli, even pictures of those objects—whether old photographs or simple mental pictures—can serve as pump-primers.

Look at Your Own Pictures

People of all ages enjoy looking at pictures and being reminded of life events. Find a favorite picture from a photo album and think about the experience it reminds you of. Notice the details in the photo, such as the expressions on people's faces, the setting, or the type of equipment being used. Try to think of details in your own experiences. Can you think where you were sitting or standing, what somebody said, or how you felt? Can you remember when this event happened? Pictures can sometimes help us remember experiences that seem to have been forgotten.

Look at Pictures with a Friend

You know how enjoyable it is to tell others of your experiences. It is also enjoyable to listen to your friends. Try getting together with a friend or two. Invite them to bring along some of their pictures so you can think aloud together about the pictures as you look at them.

Pick a time when you are not likely to be disturbed. Choose a favorite place to sit. Move a lamp, if neces-sary, so you both have good

Pictures serve as meaningful pump-primers

lighting. Round up a pen or pencil so you can make a note on the reverse side of the picture to remind yourself of what it shows. Make sure you and your friends are comfortable, and then show them your pictures, explaining what they remind you of. Be ready to listen to your friends if the pictures suggest experiences for them.

As you search for pictures to share, look for a variety of settings and activities you enjoy thinking about—for example, home, market, department store, or freight yard; a city scene, farmyard, or traffic; family groups or a movie theater crowd; children playing, dolls, baseball, or stickball.

There's no limit to the kinds of pictures you can use to stimulate memories of experiences. More examples include pictures of an old tractor, a farmhouse; an old radio, a dog with puppies, a blizzard, a beach scene, camping or fishing, an old wood stove, an iron frame bed, an old washing machine, a dining room table set for dinner for five, a streetcar, an old steam engine, a picture of FDR, a photo of Jack Kennedy, or a country church.

Mental Photographs

Experiences brought to mind as images can be as clear as pictures on a wall. It is useful to reflect for a moment on our own mental pictures so we realize how clear the images can be.

Each mental photograph, or image, takes place in an instant of time. One image joins together with many other images to recreate the whole experience. As you recall an experience you want to tell others about, try to visualize mental pictures of the experience.

Clara Paulsen shared an experience that illustrates the power of mental photographs. Notice the detail in Clara's story as she describes the scene.

"I grew up on a farm in north central North Dakota, near the Turtle Mountains, not far from the Canadian border—just 12 miles from Bottineau. There my parents, siblings, and I enjoyed many a happy time! We loved our house with its gingerbread trimmings and big screened-in porches and its big yard where we played croquet, softball, and penny sticks (or whipple). My father would push us and we'd go high on our strong swings.

One day, when I was twelve years old and my brother Cliff was fourteen, we were home alone. The rest of the family was away. A horse and buggy pulled up. Out stepped a man carrying the most interesting equipment that you can imagine. He was a traveling photographer. He wanted to take a picture of our house there on the farm. He said, 'I'll give you, as a premium, a large beautiful framed picture of the U.S. Capitol in Washington, D.C. So, innocently, we signed some papers. He took the photograph of our house and off he drove. Weeks later we received the promised picture, together with a lovely colored picture of our house in a large oval frame. Also included was a bill for $27.00!

Fortunately for us children, our parents never chided us for our childhood blunder. I still have the picture on the wall in my apartment. For me, it is a source of endless pleasure, remembering from time to time many an incident from my more youthful days."

What a vivid experience Clara recalled! Perhaps you have a picture in your mind that reminds you of a special event or a memorable day. Let's say it's a Thanksgiving Day many years ago. You may picture in your mind a favorite relative or the turkey browning nicely in the oven; or you may remember sitting around after dinner in a big overstuffed chair in the living room, feeling so full you could burst. Or maybe what you picture most is the moment you sat down at the table to eat. Can you picture where people were likely to have been sitting—dad, mother, sis, brother, an aunt or uncle, and maybe a grandparent or two? You might be able to remember where the plate of turkey was located, how you felt, or what you were thinking at that very instant—like a mental picture or a snapshot of that experience. If you start with that mental picture of the moment you sat down for that turkey dinner, other events of that day may soon come to mind. When you describe such an experience to a friend, she may also remember a special Thanksgiving.

Pictures and the mental photographs in our minds help stimulate memories of some of our favorite experiences, so they are very effective pump-primers.

HEARING

SOUNDS WE HEAR OR REMEMBER can be helpful pump-primers for stimulating memories and conversations. When you think about an old steam locomotive, for instance, you may almost be able to hear the powerful sounds of steam pushing those giant wheels—chugga, chugga, chugga—as the locomotive starts out from the station. Or you may remember the sound of the train's whistle.

If you are talking with someone about an object, try asking if the sound related to that object can be brought to mind. As you think about your own growing up, you may bring to mind some favorite sounds.

Songs

Music and songs stimulate many good memories. Memory is required to hear a song as a song, rather than just as some discon-nected notes. Whenever you listen to a song and hear it as a song, your memory is working. As we listen to a song and pay attention to what we are hearing, the rest of the song will often come to us. For example, try to remember a line from a favorite song. As you do, you may remember a few other lines of the song, and perhaps that song will bring to mind some experience or friendship. People growing up in different eras will usually be stimulated by different songs. Here are some songs that may bring back memories for people from the 1930s and 40s.

- Brother, Can You Spare a Dime
- Good Ship Lollipop
- Sentimental Journey
- Washington Post
- Stars and Stripes Forever
- Don't Sit under the Apple Tree
- It's Been a Long, Long Time

An excellent resource for songs is Wanda Willson Whitman's *Songs That Changed the World* (New York: Crown Publishers, Inc., 1969). This wonderful book is filled with all kinds of favorite songs that are sometimes hard to find. Such songs bring forth memories for other people, just as memories may come to mind for you when you hum a favorite old song of your own. You may recall where you were when you heard it, what you were doing, or what time it was. People familiar with the song may even hear Shirley Temple's voice in their "mind's ear" when they think of the song "Good Ship Lollipop" or bring to mind the sound of Bing Crosby's voice crooning "Brother, Can You Spare a Dime."

*Sheet music serves
as a pump primer*

Many people save sheet music through the years and keep it in a special place, such as in a piano bench. They may be willing to bring their sheet music for others to look at. The illustrations on the front of sheet music often stimulate reminiscing. For example, the sheet music for the song "Edelweiss Glide" stimulates Howard to remember falling asleep as a five-year-old child to the sounds of his mother playing that song on the piano in the living room.

Farm Sounds

Some objects and pictures may connect a person with life on the farm. Someone who grew up on a farm may remember the following sounds:

- Rooster crowing in the morning
- Cattle walking across the barn floor
- Meadowlark singing on a telephone line
- Brook babbling
- Cows mooing while waiting to be milked
- Wind howling outside
- Steam engine whistling off in the distance

City Sounds

City sounds are different from rural sounds. People who grew up in urban settings may not respond to suggestions of cows lowing or brooks babbling, but they could respond to memories of the sounds of city traffic, large crowds on a downtown street, or church bells ringing.

The following list may be used to help evoke memories of city life:
- A favorite neighbor's voice
- A subway train or streetcar
- A happy crowd
- Horns honking on a busy street
- Children playing in the park
- Spring baseball
- Stepping in fresh, crunchy snow
- Children playing in rustling leaves

Children playing in rustling leaves

Early Radio and TV Shows

Talking about old radio and TV shows may bring to mind favorite characters and long-cherished plots. Ask people what favorite radio or TV programs they looked forward to each week. Elders have had the collective experience of having listened to radio when that medium was the centerpiece of the times. People like to tell about their favorite radio or TV program. Following are some titles of early radio shows:

- Fibber McGee & Molly (and their famous cluttered closet)
- Corliss Archer
- Baby Snooks (with Fanny Brice)
- The Great Gildersleeve
- It's Arthur Godfrey Time
- Walter Winchell ("Mr. and Mrs. America and all the ships at sea")
- Lowell Thomas and the News ("So longggg ... until tomorrow!")
- Edward R. Murrow ("This, is London!")
- Lux Radio Theater

Classic old-time radio

Advertisement Jingles

Particular advertisement jingles from those early shows often bring forth smiles and conversation as people remember the jingles or the products advertised. Advertisements from old magazines may help people remember the jingles. Here are a few examples.

" ... the pause that refreshes without filling" (Coca-Cola®)

" Wheaties, the breakfast of champions"
    (Wheaties® breakfast cereal)

" BrylCream ... a little dab'll do ya"
    (BrylCream® hair dressing)

" Ivory Soap: 99 and 44 one-hundredths percent pure—
    it floats" (Ivory® soap)

" The sign of the flying red horse" (Phillips 66®)

" Rinso white, Rinso blue, happy little wash day song"
    (Rinso® laundry soap)

" Don't put bananas in your refrigerator" (Chiquita Bananas®)

" It's Johnson's Wax time" (Johnson's Floor Wax®)

Advertisement jingles from the media—radio, magazines, TV—generate great conversations about experiences. Invite people to an "Advertisement-Jingle Party." At the party, mention some jingles. Then invite people to brainstorm, making a list of jingles they remember. You might divide into teams with one group providing the jingle and the other trying to remember what the product was. Some pump-primer jingles you could use include the following:

" When it rains, it pours." (Morton® salt).

" ___, the one to buy in the first place." (Cross® can opener)

" Rich, rich, rich with flavor; smooth, smooth, smooth as silk;
    more food energy than sweet fresh milk." (Jell-O® pudding)

" Don't be half safe. Use ____ to be sure." (Arid® deodorant)

" See the USA in your ___." (Chevrolet®)

" ___, the beer that made Milwaukee famous." (Schlitz®)

" ___, the milk from contented cows" (Carnation®)

" Snap, crackle and pop" (Rice Krispies® cereal)

Smell

Aromas often help people remember experiences. The beauty and the richness of our memories is due, in large part, to the aromas we associate with our experiences. Reflecting on our own experience is again a useful resource for understanding ways to stimulate reminiscing. One of the most interesting recent developments in understanding how memories can be stimulated is through the sense of smell.

Aromas are associated with many of our life experiences; they add a rich dimension to life. Just thinking of some favorite aromas—freshly baked bread, a good pot roast, or freshly brewed coffee—may not only make your mouth water, but may remind you of some favorite experiences.

Fragrance of freshly baked bread stimulates good memories.
Susan and Douglas Ouimette in their family's Quality Bakery, Northfield, Minnesota.

Look at the following list of aromas. Take a few moments to enjoy thinking of any experiences they bring to mind. You may wish to add the names of some of your favorite aromas.

Aroma Pump-Primers

- Alfalfa
- Almond
- Baby Powder
- Banana
- Bayberry
- Blue cheese
- Bubble gum
- Burnt match
- Caraway
- Cedar
- Chocolate
- Cinnamon
- Cinnamon bun
- Clove
- Diesel fuel
- Dill pickle
- Egg nog
- Fish
- Fresh air
- Fried chicken
- Gardenia
- Garlic pickle
- Gasoline
- Gingerbread
- Gingersnap cookies
- Grass
- Honey
- Lavender
- Leather
- Lemon
- Lilac
- Lumber
- Maple syrup
- Menthol
- Mothball
- Motor oil
- New car
- Nutmeg
- Onion
- Orange
- Peanut butter
- Pepper
- Peppermint
- Perfume
- Pineapple
- Popcorn
- Redwood
- Root beer
- Sage
- Skunk
- Smoke
- Sweet corn
- Thyme
- Turpentine
- Vanilla
- Watermelon
- Wintergreen

Tell a friend a story that comes to mind as you think about one of the aromas. Then show your friend this list and see if he or she has an experience that comes to mind too. That will be fun for both of you.

How Do Aromas Work?

What are aromas, and how do they work? To begin with, aromas are tied very closely to our sense of taste. Remember when you had a cold and your nose was stuffed up? Then remember that you had little sense of taste when you had a cold. It's not just a coincidence that our ability to smell tasty things is related to how appetizing food seems to be. There's a link between aromas and appetite. But what are aromas?

Here's what is known. Anything that has an aroma is giving off part of itself—tiny molecules—and that's what we smell. The sense of smell, like the sense of taste, is called a chemical sense because we smell aromas by picking up the chemical molecules that the aromatic substance is giving off. That's true for freshly cut alfalfa hay, a hamburger, onion, fried chicken, a cedar chest, or any of the hundreds of things we smell each day.

Aroma Memory Tags

Many of the pleasant times we have had with friends are associated in our minds with aroma memory tags. An example of such a tag is the aroma we associate with a particular person, perhaps the person's perfume, powder, or soap. One person told us that a favorite early childhood memory was the smell of fresh sheets and towels in the wicker basket her mother used when bringing in the laundry from the backyard clothesline, after they had been hung out to dry in the sunshine.

Sometimes remembrance of an experience can lead to a memory of an aroma. For example, thinking about Christmas may bring to mind the smells of the Christmas tree, Christmas candy, fresh cookies baking, fireplace smoke, or popcorn being popped for stringing together with cranberries. It is fun to take the memory of some good experience and try to remember the aromas associated with it. Stop a moment and think of a favorite holiday. What aromas come to mind?

*Gladys and Julie Thorsheim
enjoying the fragrance
of their Christmas tree*

Certain emotional events may have become linked with an aroma smelled at the same time. When we smell that aroma again, the same emotional feeling may come back to us, though usually not with the same intensity.

Farm and City Aroma Pump-Primers

Just as we discussed different kinds of sounds from rural or city life, are there favorite farm or city aromas that come to mind? Does a particular experience come to mind when you remember those aromas?

Help some friends remember an interesting event in their lives by recalling aromas. Invite them to think about aromas from a farm or a city. Encourage them to reflect on a variety of aromas. Then invite several people to name the aromas they have been recalling. The others may describe what comes to mind as the various aromas are mentioned. Ask the participants to pay attention to the mental pictures they have when someone mentions an aroma. If there is time, people may be paired off to talk about their favorite aroma.

Touch

Many of our memories are stimulated by touching things. Everyone enjoys handling and touching objects they treasure. The touch of a favorite thing can bring back many pleasant feelings.

It is sometimes pleasant to remember what we have touched. When people wiggle their toes inside their shoes, they might remember what it was like to walk barefoot on ocean sand, through grass, or even in mud. Some things that people like to remember touching include the following:

- Smooth varnished wood
- Rough stucco
- Fuzzy fur of a kitten
- Starched cloth
- Sand
- Face of a small child

How the Sense of Touch Works

The entire skin surface contains special organs called touch receptors. Some of these receptors respond to pressure and others to temperature. They are particularly sensitive to change. If you feel a draft, your sense of touch is working well. It's interesting how our memories may even help us to recall what a drafty room felt like years after we experienced the sensation.

We also have the ability to remember our sensitivity to temperature. When we say, "The room right now feels about as cozy as I can remember its being," we show we can sense, remember, and compare temperatures.

Haptic Memory

The name given to the special memory for how things feel when we touch them, including their texture and shape, is haptic memory. Considerable research is being conducted to learn more about this fascinating form of remembering.

Experience the power of haptic memory in a group. Try the following activity with co-workers or friends before trying it with others.

Prepare a basket of oranges, one for each person in the group. Use a felt marker to put a number on each orange so it can be identified. Everyone is blindfolded so the oranges can't be seen, and then one orange is given to each participant.

The leader invites everyone to "Learn Your Orange," which means feeling the orange and trying to notice anything particular about its shape. There may be a groove, a dimple, a roundness, an elongation, or some other tactile quality that makes the orange unique. After a few minutes, the oranges are put together on the table. Then each person, while still blindfolded, tries to distinguish his or her orange by the way it feels when it is touched.

When participants think they have identified their oranges, they may take them from the pile. Others who can't find their oranges may ask to feel the oranges already claimed, just in case theirs have been claimed by someone else.

If this activity is done with no more than five or six persons, people will be surprised at how well they do. Of course, the more people there are, the more complicated the recognition task becomes. If you have a large group, divide it into smaller groups of five or six.

Memories of Touch

This story about the sense of touch was told to us by someone who had grown up on an Indiana farm.

Ears of corn

"I would take an ear of field corn and try to get the kernels of corn out. It was always hard to get the first kernel out, but after that, removing the kernels became easier. I would wiggle a kernel back and forth in the little extra space I could find, and pretty soon it would come out just like a tooth. Then the kernel next to it could be wiggled out easier—since there was the extra space from the kernel already out.

After the first row had been removed, I would take a different grip on the ear which, up to then, I had been working on with my fingers. I would use the thick part of my thumb—next to my palm—and kind of roll the row next to the empty space into the vacancy left by the first row."

Have you ever done that?

Solveig Steen reminisced about her experience as a child in Chicago, using the sense of touch as her pump-primer.

"We would play hopscotch on the cement sidewalk. It is played with squares on the sidewalk, like these. (She showed a drawing like the one at right.)

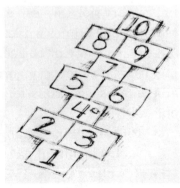

"We would find a piece of chalk, if we could. But more often than not, we would find a piece of what we called a writing stone, probably sandstone, and rub that on the sidewalk, making the lines. The sense of touch I remember is having to press the writing stone so hard in order to make a mark. I remember the vibrations and how that felt as I rubbed it across the sidewalk."

Hopscotch

Some of our most beautiful and vivid emotional memories are of experiences of touch. Dorothy Goth described this experience.

"Silent sharing is important to me. Sympathy expressed with a handclasp is comforting. Praise shown by a pat on the back may be more meaningful than effusive verbalization. Affection shown by a hug is for real. Feelings shown silently may be remembered for a long time."

VALUE OF MULTIPLE SENSES AS PUMP-PRIMERS

SOME OBJECTS PROVIDE MULTIPLE SENSE cues to prompt memories of experiences. We may see the object, hear it, feel it, and perhaps even smell it. For example, a photo of a garden in the spring may help you remember the smell of the earth, the touch of dirt, the sight of new shoots, and the sounds of the first robins. A picture of one of your old cars may evoke memories of the smell of the car when it was new, the sound of its engine, the touch of its leather seats, and the sight of it being driven home for the first time.

REMEMBERING AND REMINISCING

REMEMBERING DETAILS HELPS US INTERACT with other people. No one is born with a perfect memory, and no one develops a perfect memory. Just as we sometimes forget items we intended to pick up in the grocery store, we can also forget details from our own experiences. Memory sometimes works pretty well, but at other times it doesn't.

A great variety of objects can serve as pump-primers for reminiscing. Here are a few categories of things people like to reminisce about and some suggestions for ways to open a conversation about those objects.

- **Picture** "What a happy-looking group of people! It looks like such a beautiful day. I bet this is a special picture."
- **Jewelry** "Agnes, I've been admiring that pin you are wearing. It's such a lovely, blue color. Have you had it for a long time?"
- **Furniture** "This rocking chair feels so comfortable. It's probably had a lot of good use."
- **Book** "I noticed that you have several books about cowboys on your shelf, Frank. How did you get interested in cowboys?"
- **Food** "I see that you really like ice cream. Does ice cream taste the same now as it used to?"

- **Clothing** "That sweater you are wearing looks comfortable. Is it a favorite of yours?"
- **Music** "Every time I come in here, Rose, you have wonderful classical music playing. Have you always enjoyed good music like that?"
- **Cloth/Quilt** "That quilt over the foot of your bed has such bright colors. Tell me a little about it, Etta."
- **Aromas and Fragrance** "Mrs. O'Grady, that is such a nice perfume you are wearing. It must be a favorite of yours. Have you been using that fragrance for long?"
- **Artifacts** "What in the world is this metal ring with these wires attached? You have it on the wall, so it must be special. Where is it from, Charlie?"
- **Plants/Flower** "Every day when I come by I admire your bright red flowers. You must really like to garden."
- **Magazine** "I noticed that you get *People* magazine. I do, too. I enjoy keeping up with the people in the news. Have you always enjoyed this too?"

Tip-of-the-Tongue Phenomenon

Sometimes when we are trying to remember something, we can almost feel words there on the tip of the tongue, but we just can't get them out. Later (and it may be several days later) what we were trying to remember comes to us, even when we're not trying to think of it. In fact, sometimes it seems as though the best way to remember something is to quit trying so hard to remember it. The term tip-of-the-tongue phenomenon comes from the common phrase "It's right on the tip of my tongue, but I can't get it." The tip-of-the-tongue experience happens to all of us.

Because pump-primers are helpful when trying to remember things that are on the tip-of-the-tongue, it may be useful to review three important aspects of memory:

- Recall memory
- Recognition memory
- Attention

Recall Memory

Recall memory is remembering what you know. You work hard when you use recall memory because you don't have any clues or pump-primers to help you out. Recalling is always difficult when there are not enough clues.

By definition, recall memory is the result of searching for what you know that you know. The details in the images that you remember and see in your mind's eye are examples of your own recall memory. If you are seeing things in your mind's eye, your recall memory is working. You are remembering images stored in your memory.

As you say to yourself, "Let's see, what details were in that picture?" you are engaged in the process of recall.

Recognition Memory

Recognition memory is identifying something as familiar. The more clues there are, the easier it is to recognize something as familiar. Finding one clue will help us think of other clues that are even more helpful. The use of clues is one of the major ways pump-primers help to stimulate reminiscing. Memory clues are often in the form of pictures in our mind, such as your image of the farm scene mentioned earlier. If the clues helped you to see some details in the pictures, your recognition memory is working.

By definition, recognition memory is the result of identifying something as familiar. Recognition memory comes into play when we look at an object around us and are able to say, "That is an object I have seen before."

Recognition memory produces the feeling of familiarity we have when we see something we have seen before—it is part of priming our memory pumps. Recognition memory (identifying something as familiar) is much easier than recall memory (searching for what you know that you know), where you must remember something without any clues.

Being able to recognize something as familiar means that your recognition memory is working well, even if you need clues or prompts to identify the object. An important point to keep in mind is that it is easier to remember things if we can tie them to pump-primers.

Attention

Attention is noticing and focusing. Many people have a drawer at home where they put stuff they want to save for possible future use. Maybe you have a catch-all drawer like that. Can you picture what it looks like? Maybe there's a scissors in the drawer. Perhaps there's some string, tied together in a ball. Sometimes there's one shoelace in it, a broken pencil eraser, a couple of safety pins connected to some paper clips, and a pencil stub. There may be a little scrap of paper torn off an envelope where you've written notes long ago. All those things are in the catch-all drawer.

If you try to search for a paper clip, you may think, "Yes, I've got a paper clip, but where is it? Oh! It's in the catch-all drawer. It's too much trouble to look for it. It's as good as lost."

Lost? Yes, you think you won't find the paper clip. You don't want to go to the catch-all drawer and sort through all those things that have been collecting there. The drawer has no organization and you don't want to search for the paper clip. You would have to handle many items, asking yourself, "Is this a paper clip? No, that's that old eraser. Is this a paper clip? No, that's the pencil stub. Is this a ... ? No!" ad infinitum!

It's just too much trouble to try to retrieve the paper clip, so what many people do is give up. Although they know they put a paper clip in the drawer, they consider the paper clip lost because they know it won't be easy to find.

Our minds are sometimes like that catch-all drawer. Input goes in it randomly and continually, often when we are not paying attention.

We're certainly not going to suggest that we all ought to experience our world in an efficient, filing-cabinet way. We can't really program ourselves by saying, "Today I'm going to look only at birds and ignore everything else, and tomorrow we're going to look only at food and ignore everything else." That's impossible, of course. Instead we notice things when we see them. If we focus on them, they are stored in our memories in that order. In real life, this input is not stored in neat categories of birds, food, or people we have known.

It is helpful though to pay special attention to what we want to remember, connecting what we want to remember to some pump-primer so that later we can more easily draw out what we want to remember from our memory. Specific objects can help us to pay attention because they are easily recognized and can be an aid to helping us remember specific experiences.

~ *Chapter 4* ~

Illustrative Uses of Reminiscing

REMINISCING IS AN ENJOYABLE and meaningful activity for all people. This section describes how people in many different roles use reminiscing to affirm and enhance the sense of well-being. The examples shared here illustrate how reminiscing tools may be used effectively with people in a wide variety of settings.

We have selected stories that illustrate the use of reminiscing in six categories: caregiving, alumni and retired people, civic groups, religious organizations, medical settings, and family occasions. You may want to read first those stories that relate to situations similar to your own experiences. Take a quick look at the Table of Contents to locate the stories most interesting to you.

CAREGIVING

REMINISCING ACTIVITIES HAVE BEEN USED in many creative ways by long-term caregivers in various settings within the continuum of healthcare. You will get many ideas from their stories, as well as encouragement to adapt them in your own work. We have collected a few of their stories and put them into context categories to illustrate the broad use of reminiscence*.

---

* Where specific people and settings are described in these stories, people's real names are attached to their stories in order to credit them. In some cases, stories are composite scenarios based on collections of many similar examples we have observed in our research. We have created names and settings to accompany those scenarios in order to maintain the narrative style, and the settings and experiences are typical. In order to make clear which are specific names and settings, and which are composite scenarios, we have placed an asterisk after the names in the composite scenarios.

Creative Arts Director

"We're interested in ways to open up gateways of communication," said Bill Webb (pictured at right), creative arts director at the Good Samaritan Center in Minneapolis. As he showed us some group pictures taken by the local newspaper, Bill told us how he uses storytelling.

Bill Webb, creative arts director
University Good Samaritan
Center, Minneapolis

"The hardest part of my job is to light a fire under some individuals. It is a real sales job to get many of the residents to engage in activities that will increase their quality of life.

We must be aware of the interests and meaningful aspects of residents' lives. Reminiscing, or storytelling, helps caregivers learn what is important to the residents. It engages people who often don't participate in other group activities. Through storytelling those people often find themselves engaged in self-expression. Storytelling can happen in many ways—with the help of movement, art, music, poetry, bibliopoetry, aromas, and so on.

We feel we are providing a special approach to the state mandate for activities in facilities such as ours by building on the wellness and strengths that residents already have. We work together with the rehabilitation therapists in physical therapy, occupational therapy, and speech therapy, in what we call expressive therapy.

A local playwright was able to stimulate the residents to think of stories of their own by traveling around in a van with eight of them at a time. They visited places where the residents had lived.

We also arranged for a group of children to visit from Seward School, the elementary school several residents had attended as children. When we announced that kids from Seward School were coming, we asked if any of the residents were familiar with Seward School. One woman exclaimed, 'I went there!' When we asked her what the school had been like, she was eager to respond. 'Well, in those days, they had streetcars. I used to ride the streetcar to the Coliseum Ballroom to dance.' Her story reminded another resident of something her mother used to do to encourage her during grade school.

Storytelling is a way to help residents who are reticent and unaccustomed to group involvement to become involved in group activities."

Activity Director

Sylvia Dextore*, the activity director at a senior center, tells how reminiscing helps her become acquainted with residents.

"Mrs. Polansky was born and raised in Chicago. She moved to our community when she was seventy-two years old, a few years after the death of her husband. She is healthy and enjoys going to the senior center. But she draws a blank whenever she tries to remember recent events.

One day I visited Mrs. Polansky in her room. On the wall above her dresser was a photograph of several children; large skyscrapers loomed over the trees in the background. I said, 'Mrs. Polansky, I notice that picture on your wall. Would you tell me the story behind it?' As though my request were a spark plug to get her talking, she began to tell me that she was the little girl with dark hair and that the other children in the picture were her childhood playmates. She laughed when she recalled how she had liked the boy standing next to her and how she used to tease him. When talking about these experiences, she seemed to come to life in ways that I had not seen before.

I felt closer to Mrs. Polansky from that moment on. Later I found myself connecting some of my own childhood experiences to some of Mrs. Polansky's—like the good feeling she got when she thought about the special boy from her childhood. It brought to mind my own girlhood and a boy for whom I had similar feelings. I could relate to what she was saying and feeling.

I enjoy visiting Mrs. Polansky because I feel I know her. In fact, I learned something in that interaction with Mrs. Polansky that I have used in other situations. I now make a point of noticing an object or knickknack in a resident's room and asking about it. Doing so makes my visit more enjoyable and conversation is easier. Often something in my own experience is triggered by what the other person says, so when I have a chance to talk about my own experience, they are clearly interested. I have a good time, and so does the person I visit."

Certified Nursing Assistant

Stanley Hubertt*, who works as a nursing assistant, tells how his patients like to reminisce. Not only do the patients enjoy talking about their past, but Stanley also enjoys their stories!

"I recently drove Mr. Schmidt, one of our residents, to his old home town. The trip was a good opportunity for him to reminisce about his younger days. When we returned, Mr. Schmidt's eyes were glowing and a smile stretched from ear to ear. What a difference this short trip made in his life!

Mr. Schmidt was alert as we drove up and down Main Street and then along the side streets. He identified one of the houses as the old Olsen place and went on to tell about Tommy Olsen, his classmate in elementary school. He had enjoyed spending time over at that house with Tommy when they were boys. When I asked what he and Tommy had liked to do together, he told how they would jump from a swing in the back yard and plan fishing trips for creek chubs at the irrigation ditch that ran behind town. He described how they would go outside after a rain to collect worms. The worms would be stored in a big box filled with dirt in preparation for the next fishing trip."

Custodian

Frank Weizer* is a custodian at a senior residence center. He enjoys his frequent contact with members of the community and looks forward to hearing their stories.

"I carry a big roll of duct tape in my custodian's toolbox, and it always seems to conjure up stories. Today's duct tape serves the same purpose that bailing twine used to in the old days. I enjoy hearing the stories some of the residents tell me, particularly the men, about ways bailing twine saved the day.

I regularly go into the residents' apartments to tend to maintenance needs. I don't know ahead of time what kind of fixing is needed. I might fix a leaky faucet, reattach a bathroom tile in a shower, replace a light switch, or sand off a rough spot on the edge of a countertop. My green toolbox is my traveling workshop. In it I have a couple screwdrivers, a slot-head and a Phillips, to be exact; vice-grip pliers; hammer, electrician's tape, and some supplies for fixing leaky faucets— like gaskets. And, of course, I always have my duct tape!

Duct tape as a pump primer

Like the duct tape, my tools seem to spur comments by the residents. I hear stories about faucets that would not turn off on someone's wedding day. The men tell me how similar some of my tools are to ones they used, and they describe the repairs they used to do. I enjoy my work. The days go faster because I get to talk with these folks, and I think it's good for them too. They always seem to perk up when we get to exchange stories."

Dietary Aide

David Roberts, a dietary aide in a retirement center, tells this story about one of his residents.

"I was setting tables about 4:30 in the afternoon. A woman who had been a resident with us for some time was sitting at her usual spot, patiently waiting for dinner, which is served at 6:00 P.M. She was humming Christmas carols, looking at her purse, and folding her napkin—like she does every day.

She was humming "Silent Night" when I walked by, but paused to ask me what time dinner would be, like she did every evening. I said we would have dinner in an hour. Then I noticed she had on a green pin. It looked like it was ceramic, but it could have been stone. 'That's a nice pin,' I said, "you should be wearing that for St. Patrick's Day." She replied, 'Oh, no. I got that from a friend at Christmas. I like to wear it.'

That is all she said about the pin, but she seemed pleased. She smiled and then a few minutes later she said to me, 'Thank you for being nice to me.' Then she started humming again. Even though she did not say as much as some of the residents do, she was happy I asked her about her pin. The short interchange made both of us happy."

Long-Term Care Facility Director

Frank DeMarra* directs a long-term care facility. He has found that staff who learn to appreciate the value of storytelling begin to use reminiscing when they work with residents.

"Each week I facilitate a business meeting at the long-term care facility where I am director. Prior to the meeting, we have a talk-around. Bring-a-Thing (See Chapter 7 for a full description of this activity) is a wonderful tool to add to the talk-around. It's a good icebreaker because it quickly establishes cohesion within the group and helps make the participants less anxious. It is a good enabler for staff who might otherwise have difficulty communicating with residents. Bring-a-Thing can help spark communication. It helps build positive relationships among the staff and is a tool they have adapted for their interactions with residents."

Resident and Independent Living Coordinator

At the Earle Brown Commons Retirement Complex in Minneapolis, resident Dorothy Peters and independent living coordinator Jan Udenberg came up with an idea for storytelling in their residence. They had noticed many people sitting around, uninvolved in any activity. Dorothy and Jan decided that telling stories of life experiences might help activate people. "To be meaningfully engaged is important for all of us," Dorothy commented. "I'm glad my calendar is full; that's what keeps me going." And busy she is! At 75, she became a governor's appointee to the Minnesota Board on Aging and an at-large delegate to the Health Promotion Institute of the National Council on Aging in Washington, D.C.

Jan and Dorothy placed an announcement in "Happenings", their monthly activity calendar, inviting ten people to help them start up a story-sharing process for the retirement complex. The goal was to encourage people to talk about life experiences. The plan was to start small and then build as interest grew. Here's the story of how it came about, in Dorothy's own words.

"We decided to begin our new storytelling experience at our regular card club meeting when forty to fifty people are usually gathered together. We decided to use name tags for the meeting, with names printed in large letters since we noticed people living in this complex often did not know each other's names. Name tags help avoid the awkwardness of having to ask everybody, 'What is your name?'

People were invited to Bring-a-Thing of their own to the card-playing session. It could be a photo, a book, an article of clothing, or anything else. In the course of playing cards, people were encouraged to talk and ask questions about the things they had brought. Well, the proof is in the pudding. This has become an increasingly popular activity and the number of participants is still growing."

Grounds Crew Member

When seniors move into care centers, they often become friends with the men and women who work on the property. Watching the day-to-day tasks of mowing the lawn or weeding flowers often evokes memories of tasks the residents did many years ago at their own homes. Ralph Gonzek* tells how his days working at a care center are enriched when residents share their memories.

"For a grounds crew member like me, summer brings lots of jobs that are different from the ones I do the rest of the year, like mowing around the building, sweeping grass clippings from the sidewalk, trimming the bayberry hedge out front, and pruning the big evergreen tree next to the sidewalk.

These jobs all have what I call 'space,' time when I can easily carry on a conversation with someone even though I'm busy. I like to talk when someone comes up and says, "How's it going?" or the residents may show me they want to talk by saying something like, "What do you think about all the rain (or dry weather, and so on)?" I know they want to pass the time of day with me, and I like that.

I recall a few years ago when we really had a dry summer, one person started out saying, 'Well, it's dry, but if you really wanted to see dry, there's nothing since the summer of 1936 for dry. We had dust storms so bad the dust came in under the closed windows, and you could feel the grit between your teeth when you chewed.' Now there was a person with some experiences."

Home Health Visitor Trainer

Bill Smith* is a home health visitor who uses reminiscing in the training of volunteers who visit homebound persons. He finds it helpful to train volunteers to look for objects that can facilitate conversations.

"I tell the volunteers to ask the person they visit about an object they see in the home. If there is to be a return visit, the volunteer can bring along an object, such as an advertisement for a favorite activity, like bowling.

This technique lets the volunteer feel more comfortable by providing an opening topic. Even with the cognitively impaired, the visitor can easily begin to talk about the specific item in hand. Residents who are unable to speak have indicated in other ways that this experience is enjoyable. This is a great idea, with high congruence of process and content."

In-home Provider

Susan Roberts is an in-home provider. She told us of an experience she had with Kay, one of her elderly clients.

"All my efforts to communicate had met with failure. I would say to her, 'Kay, how are you today?' and she would respond, 'Okay, I guess.' Or I'd ask her to tell me about herself and she would say, 'Oh, I don't remember much.' Since I didn't know anything about her, I could not go much further with the conversation.

But one day I noticed a couple of old photographs lying on her table. One was a wedding picture taken by a professional photographer. The other picture was of a dog, and it looked like it had probably once hung on Kay's wall.

I picked up the picture of the dog first and held the photo so she would see it. I pointed to the dog and asked, 'Is this your dog?'

Well, you should have seen how she perked up. Right away I could see a sparkle in her eyes, and she started smiling. 'YES! That's my dog,' Kay said, with much feeling. 'I loved it so much.'

'I had a dog once too, Kay. My dog would wait for me at the top of the hill, looking for me to come home from school.'

Kay continued, 'Yes, my dog used to follow me to the door, too, and wait for us kids to come home. When it was time for my dad to go to bed (because he worked the night shift), the dog knew exactly what was happening. He would jump on the bed and sleep with my dad.'

I told Kay more about my dog and how I trained her to shake hands. Kay asked me if I had won any prizes. I told her I had never entered my dog in any contests. We had a good time sharing stories about our dogs.

After a while, I picked up the wedding picture. I didn't know who the people in the wedding party were so I asked Kay.

She looked at me with eyebrows raised. 'Well,' she said coyly, 'that's me and Tony.' With great animation, she went on to tell me how handsome her husband was. She talked and talked about her dress. 'It was just a plain ordinary dress, but to me it was beautiful.' Then she told me who made the dress and she pointed out details on the veil. She even mentioned how hot it was the day of their wedding—in November!

We must have spent twenty minutes or more chatting about her wedding and about our dogs. All this when she had never before spoken more than two words at a time to me! Because I could see her dress, I could ask specific questions about the fabric, her shoes, and the flowers. And it was fun for me to talk about my dog too. Just looking at those pictures seemed to bring back a flood of memories for Kay."

ALUMNI AND RETIRED PEOPLE

Alumni Director

During World War II many families in the armed forces lived in barracks, raising their families there. Though they retain vivid memories of a hard existence, these families who were neighbors long ago have often maintained close ties. The project described here recounts how one group of people was helped to tell stories of those days and, in the process, regained the close ties they remembered.

Marcia Baer (alumni director at the University of Minnesota—Mankato) and her partners set out to identify everyone who had lived in the barracks near the campus between 1947 and 1964, with the goal of gathering information, stories, and pictures that could be published as a book titled *The Barracks Babies*. Her account of this project contains some very helpful tips on what to include if you decide to begin a similar project.

"This project started when we published a plea for barracks information in our campus newspaper, *TODAY* at Mankato State. Letters and photos literally poured in from across the United States. Phone calls provided more leads. The interest was definitely there. People wanted to share their experiences, frustrations, and feelings about having been part of that extended family. It was a time in their lives that they wouldn't have traded for the world."

Marcia sent the following letter to project participants:

"Here's what we need: Sit down and write us a story about living in the barracks. What was life like there? Did you do things together? Did you experience natural dangers—such as rats, tornadoes, or temperature extremes? Ask your children if they have anything to contribute. Look through your old scrapbooks and send your barracks pictures. Put your name on the back of the photos; they will be carefully guarded and returned."

Elderhostel Teacher

Thomas Franklin*, an elderhostel teacher, tells about inviting participants to bring personal artifacts to class.

"Sometimes a single object, like an interesting picture of a picnic at a park, will trigger whole chunks of memory, and five other people will respond with their own stories about picnic experiences. This makes a good icebreaker at the beginning of the class."

The Breakfast Group

"We talk about our lives," said Breakfast Group member Dan Palm as he described what the group of retired teachers talks about when it meets every Tuesday for breakfast at a local cafe. They decided to meet because, although they had worked together (in some cases, for decades), they wanted to know more about one another apart from their roles as teachers.

Some members of the Breakfast Group
Joe Iverson, Gordon Rasmussen, Dick Fehner,
Keith Anderson, Cliff Swanson, Chuck Lunder,
Dan Palm, and Stan Frear
enjoying each other's company
Minneapolis Star Photo by Charles Bjorgen,
June 19, 1993, p. 1B.

The Tuesday breakfast meeting usually has a focus, which changes now and then throughout the year. For example, for several months members may share stories about their lives before they became teachers. Each Tuesday one member told something about his life. With up to thirty-five people attending the breakfast, the stories were varied and often provided new insights about group memories. Regardless of the particular focus, reports from the group are very positive. One member said, "It's one meeting I really look forward to. It's a highlight of my week."

CIVIC GROUPS

Rotary

Bill Stevens*, a retired professor, describes how his Rotary Club used reminiscence. Members were invited to bring along to the next week's meeting an old photograph they were willing to talk about.

> "On the day of the program, each person was invited to pair up with a partner. One person began telling about the picture he brought, while the other person listened. After a couple of minutes, the roles were reversed; the person who had been the teller became the listener, and vice versa.

As soon as the first person in each pair began telling their stories, the noise level in the room began to rise. People leaned toward one another to get a good look at the photo being shared.

When Dan showed Pete his photo of a tractor in South Dakota, Pete exclaimed, "South Dakota? Dan, I didn't know you grew up in South Dakota and knew farming. I grew up on a farm near Mitchell, South Dakota!"

Dan and Pete were soon talking about their memories of growing up as children on farms in South Dakota. Pete had brought a picture of the living room in the farmhouse where he had grown up. He recalled how the ceilings of the downstairs rooms had open gratings to let the heat from the oil stove rise to the upstairs. He and his siblings would sometimes lie on the floor and listen through the grates to the grown-up conversations down below, sometimes falling asleep in that position.

Later Dan reflected upon how he has discovered a new basis for friendship with Pete because of their common roots in South Dakota and how much they both enjoyed the experience."

Community Center Director

Community center directors hear many good ideas in the course of their work. Here's one example from Mary Barnes*, who directs a community center in San Francisco.

"Ruth mentioned at our weekly lunch that every box she was sorting in her basement seemed crammed with objects that brought back wonderful memories—things her children had made in school, remnants from sewing projects on which she had worked, notes from community meetings, photos from vacations up north at the lake. As Ruth was talking, it was clear that her sorting experience was shared by many at the lunch.

Someone at the luncheon commented that it would be interesting to have a program that focused on things people find as they sort through their personal belongings. The interest this idea generated was strong, so I suggested those who were interested get together after lunch to plan. Two people signed up, and they became the planning group. They each knew of two or three others who were also sorting through belongings, so they called those friends. The group met one day, and each person brought along a couple of things found while sorting through boxes. It was so much fun to talk about these objects and listen to the memories stirred up by the items that they decided to repeat their reminiscing as part of a program for other community center members. Since then we have had several programs of a similar nature involving about five people each time.

The programs are fun for the whole group. And for many, the difficult task of sorting belongings becomes more pleasant because they can share their stories."

Daycare

Adjusting to daycare may be difficult for many seniors. Darlys Springer* tells how she helps older adults feel comfortable with their new surroundings.

"We have a new daycare program. It is for physically and cognitively impaired adults who are sixty years of age and older. When a new resident is admitted, I ask the family to bring a memento that can be publicly displayed, and I incorporate that object into our monthly calendar. A different thing is featured each day, along with the name of the person who owns it. For example, one family might bring an old-fashioned skeleton key that a resident had used as a child. Perhaps the key had opened the kitchen door; now the

Skeleton key like the one identified in the daycare program

key may remind the person of the good smells he or she would often encounter when the kitchen door was opened long ago, such as the aromas of Mom's freshly baked chocolate cupcakes. The owner of the object is the focus of attention the day his or her thing is featured. As we develop our program, we will be offering services to Alzheimer's patients and their families too. We also hope to use *Bring-a-Thing* with them in some form."

Discussion Group Leader

Group leaders are always looking for new ways to begin their activities. Hap Wenger* tells how fortune-telling can make people feel comfortable.

"When I am a discussion group leader I use a process I call fortune-telling as an icebreaker. It works with any size group, but I usually put people into groups of five or six. Each person selects an ordinary object he or she has brought to the group (i.e., keys, a pencil, a pin, a purse, a receipt from a restaurant where a family celebration was held). Then with eyes closed, each person places his or her object in the center of the floor so no one will know who owns each object.

With their eyes open, people select objects from the floor that are not theirs. They study the objects they selected for a few minutes and then tell what importance they think the objects have. Each object is then claimed by its owner, who relates a story about what the object means to him or her. The process then continues around the circle."

Technology Center for Elders

Sidsel Bjørneby at the Sinsen Senior Center in Oslo, Norway, tells about helping seniors make use of new technologies.

"Our senior center has a focus around technological things that people may want to learn how to use. Examples include using computers for writing their life stories, cellular phones to call friends without having to seek out a telephone, and automatic ticket machines for purchasing subway tickets in the city. Our senior center is located in an industrial area of Oslo, Norway, and many of the users of the center have lived in the area for sixty years.

Technological systems are becoming steadily more complicated. For elder users, such technology can often lead to problems if they never have the opportunity to become acquainted with these systems. Elders often have some skepticism about new technology.

As they become involved in the use of these technological tools, people talk with one another about their families, careers, trips—experiences of all kinds. Learning to use technology and to teach others about it is important because the opportunity also provides a reason to get together and reminisce.

Our present project is a result of cooperation between the telecommunications and the human services branches of the government. We like to describe the approach that has guided the development of our project as looking at technology and elders through eyeglasses with a plus (+) sign on them instead of a minus (-) sign. What we mean by that is that we see technological advances as a resource for elders, not as a problem.

Seeing technology as an asset requires providing supports for people to learn to use these modern tools. A key in the process, however, is that the people themselves have a sense of ownership in the learning. For that reason, we have helped elders make a videotape in which they star, use the computers and cellular phones, or purchase tickets from automatic ticket machines. In this way, the elders themselves are the teachers of other elders. This technique generates lots of conversations."

Religious Organizations

Congregational Volunteer

The church remains an important anchor in the lives of many seniors. Arlys Martinson* tells how storytelling helps her as she visits elderly church members.

"One of several volunteer activities at our church is the Friendly Visitors program. As Friendly Visitors, we call on people who have difficulty getting out to attend church. I have been part of the Friendly Visitor program for about three years now. I keep doing it because I feel I'm making an important contribution to the happiness of others, and that gives me a sense of happiness. I also look forward to the enjoyable conversations I have with the people I visit.

When I visit someone who can't get to church because of a health condition, I try to bring along a copy of the church bulletin for the next Sunday's service. The bulletin helps them to follow along with the service as it is broadcast on our local AM radio station. The church bulletin always includes lots of news items people like to talk about; for example, announcements about church activities, names of people involved in the congregation, schedules for various study groups, and activities of the youth group. Often bulletin notes will bring to mind questions such as what the flowers in the chancel looked like. Sometimes people ask me about their friends that I may have seen at church on Sunday.

For some of the people who have been members for a long time, I might bring along a photo from the church archives taken during some special event, like a

Pictures on a shelf can stimulate memories

Christmas program or a congregational dinner—a photo showing lots of people. The older members can always find people they know in these photos. Sometimes they even find their own pictures.

After we talk about the church picture, people often begin to show me their own photographs that sit on pianos, bookshelves, and table-tops. They always enjoy talking about their pictures, and I am always interested in the stories they tell me."

Chaplain

Bruce Peterson, chaplain at an Ebenezer Society residence, tells how reminiscing can become part of a worship service.

"I work with a group of adults in an adult care program. About half of these people function well. The adults come from various faiths. I use reminiscing as a way to encourage people to interact with one another. I lead a twice-weekly worship service where I use Care/Share as a way to revitalize those attending. Care/Share is an activity that provides a means of talking about one's life and listening to others as they do the same.

When planning the services, I follow the church's guidelines for the lessons of the day or the texts that are used for the commemoration of festival days within the Church year. For example, on St. Joseph's Day which also honors all carpenters, a carpenter might be asked to talk about his work and life on that day. As people's experiences flow, conversation may continue for thirty minutes. This is an effective way to name things that have been a big part of people's lives.

Faith and life fit with reminiscing. Our own history is recognized when we tie it in to the history of the Church."

Christmas Sharing

For the luncheon their women's group was planning, Noreen Benson and her friends came up with a creative idea to encourage telling stories of life experiences.

"On each table were centerpieces in which we had included such things as oranges stuffed with cloves or an old doll. These items were passed around after the meal for people to look at.

Then the women broke into small groups. One person was selected by each group as its spokesperson. Each person in the group had two minutes to share her story of a Christmas memory. The women were encouraged to talk about memories of special Christmas food; an early, or particularly significant, Christmas; a Christmas program, or any other memory. Attention then returned to the spokespersons, who summarized what people talked about.

One woman said her dad would always bring home their Christmas tree on Christmas Eve afternoon because the trees were marked down then. Her dad made a stand for the tree, and they had real candles on it. She remembered how they looked forward to the tradition. Another member described her memory of learning

Jan Wallaker, Ragna Evenson, Val Fure and a friend at the Christmas luncheon

pieces to recite at the Christmas program and the bags of Christmas candy that were handed out afterwards, including clove-flavored ribbon candy, which was one of her favorites.

After the luncheon, the written evaluations were very positive. One person reflected, 'I think it was lovely hearing the memories of other people. Little pages of history! You can relate to their joys and disappointments and enrich your own memories.'

Those who worked on the program had a delightful time thinking up pump-primers for the centerpieces, taking pictures, and thinking of other creative ways we could encourage people to reminisce."

MEDICAL SETTINGS

Heart Group

Anne Jebens is a physical therapist in Oslo, Norway. She leads a group of twenty men who are open-heart surgery patients in a medical setting. The men realize that reminiscence has played a key role in their rehabilitation.

The men range from fifty to eighty years of age. They meet in the heated swimming pool of a large hospital and call themselves the Heart Group. Most have a scar running from just below their throats to near their navels. "Anne leads us in physical therapy exercises that strengthen our hearts," said Erik, one of the members who owns a store in Oslo.

Anne leads the group through a series of exercises, from leg-lifts and arm-swings to jogging in place and jogging across the waist-deep portion of the pool. Rolf, one of the group members, said, "This is most important to me. I look forward to each of the twice-weekly sessions. This is a close group of men, a group in which talking with others is easy. You see, we all have this scar."

When asked if talking meant that they talked about things related to his heart, he said, "That certainly comes up. I thought I was the only one until I saw all these other guys, each with their scars too! But we also talk about problems or family life. We joke with one another, and we just plain enjoy each others' company. We talk together about everything. It's easier for us men to talk when we are doing something else, like showering or exercising in the pool." When asked if he had always enjoyed such companionship in his life, he answered, "Never before. I talk with these men about things I never would have talked with anyone about before, particularly with men—things that are really on my mind!"

Another member said, "These men are a very important part of my life." When asked if he ever wished he had met these men earlier in his life since he enjoyed sharing stories with them so much now, he replied, "I would never have had the chance. This group has men who are really very different from each other. There is a diplomat from the State Department, the owner of a major book store in the city, a construction worker, a doctor—to name just a few. We don't talk about our professional lives, even now. We talk about things in our personal lives—stories of what's going on in our lives." When asked if he thought it was easy for men to talk about such things, he replied, "Not at all. The only reason we do is that we all either have this sign (he pointed to his scar) or will be getting one, like him over there. He is scheduled for open-heart surgery."

The man pointed out said, "Yes, I have surgery coming up soon now. At first, I was frightened of the thought and didn't talk with anyone about my fear. Then I joined this group and saw all the men that had already had the surgery and survived. I was able to talk with them about my fear. They all said they had experienced the fear beforehand too, but they are doing just fine. Now I don't feel any fear—well yes, I still have some fear, though not as much. And I can talk about the fears I do have and know that I will probably be okay too."

After the one-hour session, the group headed to the showers, joking and acting like an athletic team after a win. In the shower, the men talked about upcoming events like the hike the group was planning to take in the Nordmarka Woods outside Oslo. "We're planing a hike in the woods together," said Ivar. "I never thought I'd see the day when I would be doing that, not after heart surgery!"

"Seriously," commented Lars, a construction worker in his late fifties, "if I had realized how healthy it is to have a social support network of people I could talk with, I might not have needed heart surgery and wouldn't have this sign!"

The Heart Group illustrates how storysharing provides an opportunity for people to generate the mutual social support that is so vital for a sense of well-being. It shows that people can be helped to find common ground and share stories around anything, even overcoming the same health problems.

Blood-Pressure Clinic

Delores Mandal* is a volunteer nurse who helps at a weekly blood pressure clinic at her church. She has found that tension drops—and so does blood pressure—when people tell stories.

"Our blood-pressure clinic takes place here at church every Sunday morning from 8 A.M. until noon. We find this convenient location is a centralized place for many who would like their blood pressure monitored. But we find people often arrive after having exerted some effort to get here—such as coping with public transportation. In other words, their blood pressures may be somewhat elevated because of their physical exertion. Even a minute of conversation about something of interest to them seems to help them settle a bit. I often initiate story-sharing by making a comment about some thing they are carrying or wearing. 'That looks like a useful handbag you have there. I don't know what I would do if I couldn't have mine with me.' That usually results in some other storysharing of a friendly nature about handbags or what's in them, and the process of taking the blood pressure goes more smoothly."

Home Visit

Dr. Jan Bjørnsen, a geriatrician in Oslo, Norway, tells another story about how story-sharing is used by health care providers.

"We sometimes make home visits when home visitors alert us to possible health concerns of people living independently. It is most important that they be treated with dignity when they are visited. A relaxed conversation is a useful way to assess a number of health-related indices. A good way to begin such a conversation is to spot some object that the person has on display, such as a family picture, some needlework or stitchery, or some other thing that clearly has been saved for some reason. Persons who are functioning well invariably respond with interest to my comment about the object, such as 'This is very pretty needlework!' or 'That's quite an attractive group of people in that picture!' If someone has had an ingrained belief that they should not talk about themselves, reminiscing about some object provides a simple entrance point."

Bedside Care

Anne Weiss, a former student of ours who went on to become a physician, tells how one of her supervising physicians used reminiscence as a tool to connect with patients when she was in medical school.

> "The doctor would always begin his meeting with hospitalized patients with a conversation about some experience or another. One of his patients was an older man who used to pilot barges on the Mississippi River. Briefly the doctor would ask his patient about dangerous experiences on the barge or the impact of the ice breaking up in the spring. The discussion would only take two minutes, but clearly it was important. It allowed a warm and human relationship to develop between the physician and patient. I know it affected the health and well-being of that man."

FAMILY OCCASIONS

Aunt Molly Iron-in

A group of women in Jan Roberts' family got together after the death of their favorite aunt. Because Aunt Molly had loved ironing clothes, one of her nieces, Mary Ellen Rowe, decided to invite the women in the family to get together for what they called an *Aunt Molly Iron-in*. Each brought along an iron and an ironing board, plus some things to be ironed. The stories went on all afternoon as the women related their memories of Aunt Molly, like the wonderful aromas that came from her kitchen when she prepared German food.

This was a wonderful family activity, with participants ranging in age from first-graders to octogenarians. The younger generation learned about their family in ways they had never known. The older ones shared the stories, and a few tears too. The family tape-recorded the entire afternoon so those wonderful stories can be shared for generations to come.

Sorting through Things in the Basement

Gladys Thorsheim tells how she found special Christmas gifts for her family and how this created a reminiscing activity for the whole family.

"Last Christmas, I was puzzling about what gifts to get for my adult children. I wanted them to know how much I still cherish them and their families. One day when I was doing the hard work of sorting through boxes of things in the basement, an idea came to me.

It was taking a long time to sort through things we had put in boxes and saved over the years—things like the kids' first toys, my late husband's tools, and stones picked up on vacations here and there. Well, the reason it was taking so long was partly that each thing was loaded with good memories and I just enjoyed sitting back, fondling the objects, and bringing to mind the sweet memories they stirred in me.

Why not wrap up some of these things and give them to the family, along with a note saying I would like to tell the story behind the memento? I even wrote myself a reminder of what I particularly wanted to share about each thing. So that's what I did last Christmas. The kids and the grandkids were pleased to get the things as mementos—and even more pleased, it seemed, to listen to me tell the story about each object. And I enjoyed every minute of it too!"

Family Birthday Things

Ruth Adams*, a mother of young children, decided to celebrate the birthday of her oldest son, Mark, in a unique way.

"I began by asking my other children and husband to bring things to the dinner celebration that reminded them of Mark. The things ranged from well-worn favorite books to some remaining pieces of the blanket Mark had as a young child; from a miniature tea set used for late-night tea parties in a closet when the parents were sound asleep to baby teeth saved by the tooth fairy. It was an occasion filled with laughter and remembrances."

~ *Chapter 5* ~
Pump-Primer Ideas

THE *THING* ALCOVE

CHUCK AND DEANNA SANDSTROM have what they call their *thing alcove* next to their front door. In the alcove, they have arranged several objects from their childhood. Chuck has an American Flyer electric train locomotive and coal car sitting on two pieces of track. Deanna displays her old Chinese checkerboard. There is a toy car that Chuck made long ago for their daughter, with its round wooden wheels fashioned from a broomstick. Also waiting to be noticed are Chuck's father's violin, a couple of houseplants, and a toy muppet. These things have meaningful connections for three generations in their family and are instant conversation pieces when people drop in.

Chuck Sandstrom showing their alcove thing

In the picture above, Chuck is explaining how, as a boy, he loved to watch his locomotive produce smoke. Liquid smoke was squirted into the smokestack. As the train warmed up, a heating element inside the smokestack would vaporize the liquid smoke, producing puffs of smoke as the train went around the track.

Displaying objects in your home is a good way of stimulating your visitors to have an interesting conversation. By showing things that have been important in your life, you are telling people what is important to you—you are also setting the stage for reminiscing.

Think about the objects on your tables and bookshelves. Change them periodically—so you too can reminisce about different objects.

The clothing and jewelry you wear may also give the people you meet an idea about what is important to you. When someone asks about your necklace, use the opportunity to reminisce! More than likely the listener will think back to a similar story in his or her past, and soon you will both have enjoyed reminiscing.

Make a habit of looking for things that are important to others. Notice jewelry. Ask about key rings. Take time to look at photos and other objects that are on display in someone's home. You are giving a gift when you initiate a conversation that centers on something meaningful to another person. In response, it is likely that person will want to give a similar gift back to you, and soon you may be telling your own story.

Residents at an assisted living center in Kalmar, Sweden, have another way of exhibiting their mementos. At the front entrance of the center, display cases show off objects residents once had in their homes. These displays are changed every month. Often included are items of clothing, which are displayed on mannequins.

INVITE PEOPLE TO TALK
ABOUT THEIR COLLECTIONS

IDENTIFY SOMEONE WHO HAS A COLLECTION, and create a story-sharing session based on the collection. If Anne has a collection of dolls from around the world, dressed in their colorful native costumes, ask her if she would be willing to bring a few of them to share at a gathering. Explain that others may find them interesting.

After Anne's presentation, invite people to talk with their neighbors about dolls they have or remember having.

In this way, everybody will have a chance to talk about memories that were stirred as Anne showed her dolls. These informal conversations often allow people to learn things about their neighbors. After a pump-primer activity, conversation is usually easy and helps people develop confidence in their communication skills.

Adapt this general idea to fit your circumstances. Many people have collections that can serve as pump-primers for conversations—collections of dolls, antiques, pictures of tractors or cars, or travel photos. The process can be repeated, using different collections each time.

Start a Reminiscing Class

Mary McCall had the task of building bridges between disparate groups in a building complex. The facility included an independent-living wing and a personal-care wing. "The building residents had been involved in a lot of stereotyping of one another," Mary said. "Some people in the independent living wing had said things like, 'They must be demented if they are in personal care!'"

Mary organized a reminiscing class and intentionally included people from both the independent-living and the personal-care wings. During the first reminiscing activity, one person happened to say, "Oh, I live in personal care!" "Really?" another replied, somewhat astonished. "You're not like those people in personal care."

As a result of the reminiscing class, group members began to stand up for each other when their friends would ask, somewhat critically, "Why were you talking with those people from the personal care wing?"

Mary shared her appraisal of what happened. "Usually reminiscing is considered to be an activity that benefits the individual, not the whole community. But reminiscing helps people find common ground. It's a great way to bring people together who aren't getting along. That helps the whole community."

Here are some ideas based on Mary McCall's ten-week reminiscing session. You can select parts of it for a shorter series.

Week 1: People introduce themselves and tell a little about themselves. Ground rules are established.

Week 2: People draw pictures or floor plans of the first house they lived in. If drawing or sight is problematic, people may be asked to think about their first home. Conversation is initiated by asking questions such as "Who was in the family?" or "What were your earliest family memories?" People go around the circle telling their stories.

Week 3: Focus on school experiences, including successes and failures. Encourage people to talk about topics such as their sense of identity, their industriousness or lack of motivation, or messages they received from teachers.

Weeks 4-9: Focus on any other topics people want to talk about.

Week 10: The last week is a time to bring conversations up to the present. Use pump-primer questions like "Where are you now?" or "What's on your mind now that feels important?"

TAKE A FIELD TRIP TO AN ANTIQUE STORE

THREE ACRES ANTIQUE STORE is located in a picturesque old brick firehouse in Northfield, Minnesota. "Everybody finds something that connects with their own experience when they come in, regardless of their age," said Donovan Parker, owner of Three Acres Antiques. Shoppers reminisce as they browse through the store. They talk about how they once had an item like this or used one like that; or they remember seeing an object like the

Don Parker looking over some interesting objects in his antique store

one on the floor or hearing about a piece like the one lying in the corner. The antique might be a hand-cranked ice-cream maker, a Velvet tobacco tin like Gramp had, or dishes like Grandmother used.

Parker enjoys listening in on the many interesting conversations in his store.

> "One Saturday three people came in—a grandmother, her adult daughter, and her granddaughter. The grandmother pointed to a kitchen tool and said to her granddaughter, "I used one just like that. Can you guess what it is?" As I stood to the side and listened, there was a wonderful conversation between the three generations about what it was like to work in a kitchen equipped as they were in those days."

Arrange for a field trip to a local antique store. Find a time when the store is less busy so your group will not interfere with regular customers. Speak with the owner in advance and explain that you are trying to provide a way for people to see things that connect with their own experiences as a way to prime their conversation pumps.

When you make the trip, ask people to make written or mental notes of what they see that was of interest to them. When returning home for refreshments, or at the next gathering, pair people up to share what they found to be interesting in the antique shop. Then invite the pairs to share what they talked about with the larger group.

PLACES TO USE REMINISCING ACTIVITIES

REMINISCING ACTIVITIES CAN TAKE PLACE in a variety of settings. At senior citizen centers and clubs where some are reluctant to speak up, reminiscing activities empower even shy individuals because they see that everyone is sharing memories. AARP meetings, community festival events, or retired work groups of all kinds are good places for reminiscing activities. Sharing stories is a way for people to connect at teacher meetings, administration sessions, adult classes, and professional conferences.

Reminiscing activities can break the ice at meetings to welcome new neighbors, thereby enhancing a sense of support within the neighborhood. Think about using reminiscing activities at extended family gatherings and reunions; singles meetings; individual, group, and family therapy sessions; staff meetings and training sessions, or interagency collaboration meetings. Reminiscing is always an important part of student and alumni gatherings. Church meetings of all kinds—of committees, women's or men's groups, church senior organizations, new-member groups, and even the church choir—all provide good settings for reminiscing.

Organizational development consultants may use reminiscing activities as a means of team-building within the corporate world, especially when there has been difficulty creating team spirit between different departments. Reminiscing activities can be used to open seminars, conventions, retreats, or even sales group meetings.

~ *Chapter 6* ~

Useful Tips for Reminiscing

STORIES ARE MORE INTERESTING when details are added. Sometimes a storyteller has difficulty embellishing the story, but an active listener can help. This section describes a potpourri of tips and suggestions you may use to encourage others to continue reminiscing.

USING FOLLOW-UP PARAPHRASES AND QUESTIONS TO ENCOURAGE STORYTELLING

AFTER THE PERSON TALKS ABOUT AN OBJECT, a good listener will add a comment or ask a question. You might paraphrase what has been said to make sure you got it right or to signal your friend that you were really listening. Or you might ask a question to encourage more conversation about the story. You could say something like, "That's really interesting, Chet. Tell me more!" or "What do you remember most about that experience, Ruth?" or "Tell me more about how you did that, Mrs. Johnson."

USE OBJECTS TO STIMULATE REMINISCING

IF YOU ARE A HOME-CARE PROVIDER, you might suggest to the people you visit that they should think ahead about something they would like to show you on your next visit. Moving an object out of a collection or placing a photograph in a special place will set the stage for reminiscing. Fascinating stories can even be told about the places mementos are kept, such as piano benches, boxes under the bed, or well-worn suitcases. Correspondingly, people living at home may invite visitors to bring along a craft project or an object of interest so the two can talk about the visitor's interest.

Let's say that you are walking down the hall past Ruth's room. You notice some things she has saved. You walk up to Ruth, smile, and say something like, "Ruth, I noticed that picture of you on your wall when I stopped by the other day. Is there a story behind that? Sometime when you have a moment, I'd like to hear about that picture."

Now suppose that Ruth walks over to the picture, points to it, and says, "That's a picture of me holding my oldest grandson on his first birthday.... " (And then Ruth goes on to tell more about the occasion.) Notice Ruth's interest and delight in being invited to tell the story behind the picture. Not only have you encouraged Ruth to reminisce a bit about something important to her, but you have also made it clear to her that she is doing something interesting for you as well! That is empowering.

Let's say you and Jim are talking about favorite vacation memories from child-hood. You might say, "Jim, do you have any mementos from those vacations?"

Perhaps Jim responds with a story about saving stones. He may show you a wallet-sized picture he keeps in his bill-fold because it reminds him of the smooth stones at the lake.

Now you have a chance to paraphrase what Jim just told you. You could say, "So

Wallet picture of beach stones

you have saved stones from your trips to the lake. You especially liked the round flat stones you've saved because they remind you of your father teaching you to skip rocks across the water."

Notice how Jim listens carefully as you paraphrase his story. His interest in recalling those memories will probably increase. He may elaborate about a particular occasion or a special moment he remembers. The reminiscing will be meaningful to you both.

USE BODY LANGUAGE TO SHOW INTEREST

WHEN TALKING WITH SOMEONE, even subtle body language can be used to show interest. Note in the following picture how the people are leaning toward each other and how they are looking directly at each other. Both gestures are important body language clues that people are interested in the conversation. Be aware of your body language while you reminisce.

HELPING PEOPLE LINK WITH ONE ANOTHER

Richard Stevens and Liv Hertsgaard, active listeners

ONCE YOU HAVE HAD SOME EXPERIENCE using reminiscing one-on-one, you are ready to use it as a conversation link within a group of people. This is a fun way to spread reminiscing around. All that is required for taking this step is to remember something a person has told you about their interests. Then as you hear another person talk about a similar interest, you can connect the two. It's easy. Let's look at an example of how it could work.

FINDING COMMON GROUND

LET'S ASSUME YOU AND MARY have already done some reminiscing together. You have talked about how both of you like recipes and cooking, especially desserts. One day when you asked Mary about the bowl of fresh strawberries you saw in a picture on her dresser, you learned that she loved to garden.

You have also had a few good conversations with Arthur, a neighbor of Mary's. You have noticed that Arthur greets Mary when they pass each other, so you figure they at least know each other. The next time you are talking with Arthur, he happens to mention the big garden he had in his backyard. He goes on to tell how he misses seeing things grow that he planted. Remembering how Mary also likes gardening, you might suggest that Arthur talk to Mary about their common interest.

"It's interesting that you enjoy gardening so much, Arthur. Mary and I have fun talking about recipes. I tried one of her favorite desserts just last week. It was a delicious strawberry shortcake. Mary also told me that she used to have a garden every summer and raise

strawberries. You ought to see the picture she has of some strawberries from her garden. You can just imagine how a garden that
produced such great berries must have looked."

Then, with a note of encouragement, you say,

"Arthur, you might ask Mary if you could see that picture of hers
with the strawberries from her garden. Tell her about your garden
and what you liked to grow."

Follow up that conversation a couple of days later and ask Arthur if
he has had a chance to talk to Mary about gardening. If he says,
"Nope, haven't had a chance yet," you can be helpful by asking Arthur
if he would like to go with you so both of you see Mary's picture. We
all need encouragement at times. Often it helps to go with somebody
to do something, even to do things we enjoy.

Once Mary and Arthur connect on their interest in gardening, their
common ground of experience can help keep that friendship strong
and beneficial.

Even First Attempts Can Have Benefits

There are hundreds of ways to link people through their reminiscing, but you will probably not be successful every time you try.
In the example above, Arthur may not have wanted to talk about gardening with Mary and may have said no to your request. Don't let
such a refusal discourage you from trying again.

No matter what the outcome, remember that you did accomplish
something important when you tried to link Mary and Arthur through
their common interest in gardening. You showed Arthur how you had
developed a friendship with Mary because of your shared interest in
recipes. You also demonstrated an important part of reminiscing—
talking together about shared interests.

Perhaps gardening had not been enough of a common interest to
link Arthur and Mary in conversations, but something else may do it.
Eventually, for instance, you might help them discover that they both
love dogs or that they both enjoy current events. If so, they may enjoy
sharing dog stories or talking about current events. You never know
what experiences are going to be meaningful enough to connect people. Just keep listening and linking.

CREATING A SENSE OF COMMUNITY

THE LINKS YOU HELP ESTABLISH AMONG PEOPLE, such as those we discussed above, are the way all communities begin. As friendships develop among people, an important sense of community will begin to grow. When bonding develops within a community, the personality of the community can become more positive and welcoming.

Here is a story we heard several years ago from Marilyn, a woman known for her skill in linking people together. Marilyn occasionally visited some of the elders who were members of her church. We asked her to tell us about her visits.

> "I often visited an older woman from my church. Over the years I had become good friends with her. One day as I was talking with another older couple, I noticed the couple reminded me of my friend. I gave the couple my friend's name and telephone number and told them that I thought they would enjoy meeting one another. After a month or so they called her up. Now they are good friends."

As we heard Marilyn tell us what she did, it wasn't at all clear to us what made her think the couple and her friend might enjoy one another's company. We asked her how she knew they might have some common interests. She said,

> "I guess I saw how both the women talked about their grandchildren with a sense of humor. All three were friendly people, and they all had pictures of their homes in their rooms. I sensed that they had things in common."

When we asked Marilyn how she knew if her suggestions for linking up worked out, she said she often checks back with people. She asks them if they have made the contacts she's suggested. But often without any prompting, people come back to her and say that they have introduced themselves to the other person and that the new friendship seems to be working out well.

~ Chapter 7 ~

Group Reminiscing Activities

BRING-A-THING™ ACTIVITY FOR YOUR GROUP

A BRING-A-THING ACTIVITY HELPS PARTICIPANTS tell about a thing, an artifact, or an experience that is meaningful to them. This group activity helps each participant identify his or her story, tell the story, and be heard by others.

These special objects enable people to think about themselves—their families, homes, vacations, talents, and special concerns. When people think about objects that are special to them, they take time to reflect on what is important in their lives.

Paul Anderson tells about a Norwegian weaving displayed by Meg Peck

When these ideas are shared, people learn about each other and begin to understand what makes people the way they are.

During a Mother's Day party at Fairlawn Good Samaritan Health Center in Portland, Oregon, activity director Linda Mittleider encouraged residents to bring things to the party that were meaningful to them. Many of the residents did just that. Three brought wedding dresses, several brought old photographs of their family and children, and others brought interesting mementos. The wedding dresses were hung up; the photos and other objects were placed on a table. The residents and their guests swarmed around the photos, mementos, and wedding dresses. They talked among themselves and they asked questions of the residents who brought the items. They shared stories as they looked at and touched the things on display. There was an excited and happy mood in the air as participants shared their experiences with each other.

Here's how *Bring-a-Thing* works.

- People pair up.
- One person talks for a few minutes about his or her thing; the other partner listens.
- The listener shares what he or she heard.
- People switch roles. The listener now becomes the teller, and the teller now becomes the listener.
- As before, the teller talks for a few minutes about the story behind his or her thing and the other partner listens.
- As before, the listener shares something that he or she heard the teller talk about.
- At the conclusion, people may wish to share with the larger group what they talked about in their pairs.

Leo Bjorlie and Ralph Rolland enjoying stories at a Bring-a-Thing activity

How to Publicize the Activity

The sample on the following page is a notice that could be printed in a newsletter or enlarged as a poster.

YOU ARE INVITED TO BRING-A-THING

Come with an object you are willing to tell another person about—
anything that reminds you of an enjoyable experience, for
example, a photo, a stone, or a special memento of any kind.

YOU WILL BE ABLE TO
- Use the object to get to know other people
- Tell your story
- Exchange experiences

DATE: _____

TIME: _____

PLACE: _____

Renza Anderson and Michele Malotky
enjoying a Bring-a-Thing activity

The Meeting Place

Here are some important factors to bear in mind when selecting the setting for a Bring-a-Thing.

- Choose a comfortable place with good lighting and movable, comfortable chairs. Space should be adequate so people will not be distracted by the conversations of others.

- Choose a place where it is easy for people to hear one another. Desirable places have carpeting on the floors or curtains on the windows that help keep noise to a minimum. Hearing is also aided if there is a minimum of background noise (such as fans, blowers, or machinery) that could block out the sounds of other voices.

The Preparations

Before the group meeting takes place, the leader should organize the materials for the party.

- Name tags make it easy to learn people's names. When participants fill in their own names, they can decide for themselves whether they feel more comfortable being called by their first or last names. Use large marking pens so the names can be read easily. Leaders should wear name tags too.

Another idea is to invite people to put the names of their home state or home town on their name tags so those with common roots can link up.

- Paper and a pen or pencil will be needed so each participant can jot down ideas.
- Refreshments always make a party better!
- Prepare overheads if you feel they will help to guide the activity along. These are illustrated in boxes in the following activities and can also be reproduced from Appendix 2 for use in your reminiscence program.

Confidentiality

The issue of confidentiality is an important one. Participants need to feel comfortable when they are telling their stories. It helps, therefore, to make sure that all participants know ahead of time that they will be telling others about the thing they bring.

How to Do the Activity

Step 1: Form Pairs　　　　　Takes about four minutes

Distribute supplies, including copies of the Bring-a-Thing Personal Story Record for people to use. You will find it in Appendix 1. Following are suggestions for describing each step to participants. Feel free to use these exact words if you wish.

> Welcome to our Bring-a-Thing Party. We hope you will enjoy telling about the object you brought and learning about the objects others have with them. We think you will find that this is an enjoyable way to learn about others—and you will probably gain some new insights into your life and what is important to you.
>
> For this activity, we will divide into pairs. How you form pairs isn't critical. You could count off or draw names from a hat. One partner will listen while the other tells about the thing he or she has brought. Later we will change roles.
>
> Everyone will need a pen or pencil and a piece of paper.

Step 2: Think about Your Object

Takes about five minutes

The second step may be described as follows:

If you brought a thing to talk about, that's great! But if you did-n't, you can talk about something meaningful that you picture in your mind. Or you might have something in your billfold or purse. Feel free to use that. You can also talk about something you are wearing, such as an article of clothing; a piece of jew-elry; or your shoes, ring, or watch.

Before you begin talking with your partner, please jot down a few words about the thing you brought with you. Perhaps you want to tell where your object came from or why it reminds you of a special experience—a holiday, vacation, or birthday. Maybe your object brings to mind a particular person. Topics will vary widely because all of you have different things and each thing brings you different memories.

If members of your group have trouble writing, encourage them to picture in their mind's eye an object and to think of what they want to say about it. If some participants have dif-ficulty seeing their partner's object, you may invite them to touch or smell the object.

Use your notes to help you remember what you wanted to talk about.

We will use about five minutes for this step. I'll let you know when the time is up.

If people seem to want more time and if your program allows it, feel free to extend the time. If people finish this step before the time is up, move on.

Step 3: Name Your Story

Takes about one minute

You can use the following words to describe Step 3:

What was on your mind as you were thinking about your *thing*? If you were to give a title or name to the story you were just thinking about, what would it be? For example, if you were thinking about how the stone you brought reminds you of when you first found it on vacation, you might name your story for that occasion. The title will serve as a handle for remembering later what each person's story was about.

We will take a minute for you to name your story.

If writing is difficult for your group, encourage participants to think of a title. The title will help both the storyteller and the listener to remember the topic.

Step 4: Tell Your Partner about Your Story

Takes about three minutes

You may use the following directions to describe Step 4:

Now you will get together with your partner. One person will begin. Tell the listener the name of your story. Look at the notes you wrote and begin to tell your partner about your object. Limit your story to three minutes.

The listener has a very important task. In addition to learning something about the storyteller, an active listener helps the speaker feel more like talking. We like to talk when we know someone is listening.

As a listener, you are not listening for advice or for answers to your questions, but rather you are listening to understand the talker, to understand where he or she is coming from. Your job as a listener is important.

This is a key: Your job is to keep the speaker talking for the full three minutes. You can do that by asking open questions. Open questions are questions not easily answered by yes or no. An example of an open question is "Would you tell me what items you make with that tool?" or "Would you say more about the wedding?" Active listeners also maintain good eye contact.

I will keep time and let you know when the three minutes are up. You can start now.

It may be helpful for two leaders to demonstrate the speaker and listener roles. Show how to listen actively and ask open questions.

Step 5: Tell Back Takes about two minutes

Directions:

The listener will now tell back something about what the teller said. You don't have to repeat the entire story. Once again, the person who is now listening has an important task. During the telling back, open questions may again be helpful. For example, if the person stops telling back after thirty seconds and says, "That's all I remember!" you can help by saying, "Could you say more about where I found this object?" That will help the person to recall what you said.

As you were telling your story, your partner learned something about you. As your partner tells your story back to you, your partner will begin to understand more thoroughly what is important to you and you will know that your partner was really listening.

I will keep time and let you know when the two minutes are up. You can start now.

Step 6: Learn about Your Partner

Switch roles and repeat Step 4 and Step 5.

Takes about five minutes

Directions:

It is now time to switch roles. When you switch roles, you will learn about your partner through listening to his or her story.

We may have had little opportunity to develop our own skills in listening to others for the purpose of understanding something about them. Without such listening for understanding, we tend to consider people more as objects, perhaps keeping them at arm's length.

Please switch roles now. (Repeat Steps 4 and 5.)

While participants are repeating steps 4 and 5, the leader needs to prepare for the final part of this activity. People involved in a *Bring-a-Thing* activity are often interested in the variety of things other people in the room have been talking about. While the pairs of listeners and talkers are sharing, keep an eye out for pairs that seem to be having a lot of fun. Casually approach three or four such pairs, squat down next to each pair, wait until they acknowledge your presence, and say something like the following:

"Excuse me. When people are sharing the things they brought, they are often interested in the variety of things other people are talking about. I am asking a few people if, in a little bit, they would be willing to tell something about what they talked about. Would one or both of you be willing to do that? Whatever you would choose to share is up to you. There will be several others helping out in this way."

They usually say, "Sure!" Or perhaps one partner will agree and the other will say something like, "You go ahead." Of course, if neither person seems to want to share with the larger group just say, "That's fine. Thanks, anyway," and ask another pair.

Step 7: Summarize   Takes about six minutes

Directions:

> When people do this Bring-a-Thing activity, they are often interested in the variety of objects others talked about. So while you were talking, we asked a few people if they would be willing to share what they talked about for just a minute or two. Hearing people's stories helps us tap into additional memories and issues that are meaningful to us.

Gesture toward the people who agreed to share with the group. If you have a microphone on a long cord, move over to them and give them the microphone so they have a sense of control. After they have shared, continue with the others who have agreed to talk.

Step 8: Evaluate the Activity   Takes about five minutes

People often like to have some way of evaluating an activity. You may, therefore, choose to duplicate and distribute copies of one of the Activity Evaluation Forms in Appendix 1 and invite people to fill them out.

Step 9: Break for Refreshments

Talking with Each Other   Takes about thirty minutes

Directions:

We will have refreshments now, but we hope you will continue to share with one another. Ask other pairs what they talked about.

As we have refreshments, we can continue to practice listening skills. Just like we practiced in the activity, we may help each other talk by asking open questions, that is, questions not easily answered yes or no. Whatever you choose to talk about is up to you.

What to Do When the Activity Is Completed

Once you have tried the Bring-a-Thing activity, ask your group what they would like to do next. Together you may decide to try another activity in this book or perhaps think up new activities appropriate for your group. You might repeat the activity with different things and different experiences.

BRING-A-THING
FINDING COMMON-GROUND ACTIVITY

A BRING-A-THING ACTIVITY can help your group meet a new group. Participants will enjoy meeting new people. You might invite groups from neighboring community centers or churches, residents from another floor in a residential center, school children, or visiting international students. Plan your event in partnership with representatives of participating groups. It may be helpful if representatives from each participating group share leadership responsibilities.

Here's an idea: Suggest to members that they bring the same Bring-a-Thing object they have used before. They will already have talked about it and, in a way, rehearsed what they like to say about it. It is always fun to tell about your *thing* to someone who has fresh ears. Participants in your *Bring-a-Thing* activity will learn from their differences and appreciate their similarities.

International students preparing to share food

Planning

It may have been a long time since some older persons have been in group activities with persons they have not met before. You may wish to help them feel comfortable by first introducing yourself. Tell them something about your home town or about yourself so they will begin to feel comfortable about sharing information.

How to Publicize the Activity

A flyer similar to that printed on page 75 can be distributed to publicize the activity.

HOW TO DO THE ACTIVITY

Step 1: Form Small Groups   Takes about two minutes

The following directions may be used to explain Step 1. When you have given directions, distribute supplies.

> Please help arrange the chairs into circles. We want to form groups of about four or five people each. Everybody will need a pen or pencil and some paper.

Step 2: Learn More about Yourself

Directions: Takes about five minutes

Think about what you would like to share with members of your group about the object you brought. Jot down a few sentences to help you remember the important points. By writing down a few words about this object—or what it reminds you of—you have a chance to say to yourself, "This is important to me."

You may choose to put your name on the paper so others can learn of your interests.

Instead of asking people to write, you could ask them to picture in their mind's eye what they might like to tell about.

Step 3: Name Your Story

Directions: Takes about one minute

Look at what you wrote for the last step. Think of a short name for the story you will be telling that will help you and others remember what it is about. For example, if you wrote or thought about an experience of writing letters, you might name your story "A Letter from a Friend." If you enjoy woodworking as a hobby, you might name your story "Making Wooden Toys."

We don't always think of what we do as an experience, but just as something we do. By giving the story a name, our experience is highlighted in our minds as real. We sense the importance of what we do because of the people and feelings that are part of it.

Step 4: Learn More about Each Other

Directions: Takes about ten minutes for groups of five

One person will begin by reading the name of his or her story. The storyteller can wait a moment or two while the others write it down.

Then tell your story. Don't take more than two minutes per person so there is enough time for each person's story.

Step 5: Reflect

Directions: Takes about three minutes

Look at the story titles you wrote down.

Jot down a word or two that will remind you of an experience of your own that was brought to mind while you were listening to your partner talk.

Step 6: Discover More about Your Own Experiences

Directions: Takes about three minutes

Look at the reminder words you jotted down. Choose one of those words, and write some other thoughts about your experience. You will be sharing these thoughts aloud with someone else.

Step 7: Learn About What You Have in Common

Directions: Takes about ten minutes

> Go around your group one at a time and tell the others what you were thinking about when you wrote down your reminder word. As we share, you may discover some interesting connections with people around you!

Step 8: Evaluate the Activity   Takes about five minutes

Distribute the Activity Evaluation Form in Appendix 1 to the group. Feel free to modify the form to fit your needs.

Step 9: Refreshment Break

Talking with Each Other about Things in Common

Directions:

> We'll have refreshments now. This is a good time to find out about the things talked about in other groups.
>
> It is also a good time to practice our listening skills. Just like we practiced in the activity, help each other talk by asking open questions, that is, questions not easily answered by yes or no. Ask questions like "Would you tell me more about your stone?" or "Can you tell me about some of the people in that photo?"

If the writings from Step 6 are posted on the wall, participants can be invited to meander around and read what others have written. Some groups have saved these papers for making a master list of people and their interests. They use this list later to help link people with others having common interests and experiences.

International students, wearing national dress, at a Bring-a-Thing

Occasionally, groups place their things on a table for all to see and talk about during refreshments. Make sure the owner's name is on the object so people will know who to talk with about it. Masking tape works well for this. Be sure to remove labels after the session to avoid damage.

THE BOX-O-THINGS™ ACTIVITY

THE BOX-O-THINGS ACTIVITY SERVES AS A PUMP-PRIMER for remembering experiences that are long forgotten. In the Box-o-Things activity, the facilitator fills a box with a variety of items: tools, cooking equipment, toys, keys, records, pictures, fishing equipment (without the hooks), coffee mugs, rocks, picture postcards, toys, and so on. Sometimes a local antique store is willing to lend a variety of items for the purpose. Each participant looks into the box and draws out an object that somehow rings a

A Box-o-Things

bell, bringing back memories from the past. Although the objects do not belong to the participants, these common items can still help people tap into important memories.

"I have used activities described in this book for about four years on an in-patient gero-psych unit in St. Joseph's Hospital in Lexington, Kentucky," said social worker Gail Wilhorn. "I use the Box-o-Things approach because we usually do not have access to the patients' own objects. I bring in antiques and objects from the past. One advantage is that the patients can continue with their conversation after my thirty-minute group has ended. Nine times out of ten, they are still chatting after I have gone."

Preparing for Box-o-Things

In preparation for this activity, find a box. A shoe box will do nicely. Put into it a variety of things you may have lying around the kitchen or garage or use stuff from your neighbor's attic—the more unusual, the better.

Tailor the types of things you choose for the Box-o-Things to fit the people whom you expect in your group. What might be especially interesting for a group of women may be different from the pump-primers chosen for men. Items in the box might all relate to a theme, such as the state fair, railroads, homes, pets, cooking, music, fashions, work life, World War II, summertime, automobiles, seasons, farm days, the Depression, school days, or Christmas.

How to Publicize the Activity

Include a notice like the following in a newsletter or on a poster:

> # COME SEE WHAT'S IN THE BOX-O-THINGS!
> ### *Refreshments Provided*
>
> In our *Box-o-Things* are many interesting mementos to look at and talk about—objects we have used in our hobbies and at work or play.
> Take a look into the box and see what things interest you!
> We'll have some interesting times talking together about the things that interest us.
>
> **DATE:** _____
>
> **TIME:** _____
>
> **PLACE:** _____

How to Do the Activity

1. Bring the Box-o-Things you have prepared.
2. Arrange the chairs in a circle so all participants can easily see each other.
3. Explain to the participants that you are going to pass around the Box-o-Things. Each person can choose one item that seems familiar. It should be some thing the participant is willing to tell a story about.
4. After the box has been passed around the circle, ask participants if they need more time to think of a story about the thing they selected.
5. Tell participants that each person has a limit of three minutes and that you will keep time. (Time limits may vary according to your schedule, but it is important to have some kind of limit so that a few people do not monopolize all of the time available for this activity.)

6. Then go around the circle and invite each person to tell a story about the thing he or she selected from the Box-o-Things.

7. If there is time at the end, you may want to open up the conversation so that people can talk about somebody else's thing. But what is most important is that you ensure that each person initially has had a chance to talk.

8. If, by chance, you follow this activity with refreshments or coffee, invite each person to place his or her thing on a table. As participants handle the things, they will talk informally with each other about more memories generated by the objects.

A great number of things designed especially for use in this type of activity are available commercially. For example, BiFolkal Productions of Madison, Wisconsin, carries numerous items that can serve as pump-primers. These include sets of slides, audio tapes, videos, games, and kits that combine an assortment of items. BiFolkal Productions' address is listed in Appendix 3.

THROW A BRING-A-THING PARTY™!

A BRING-A-THING ACTIVITY IS A NATURAL and meaningful ice-breaker for a party. The activity works well as a means of introducing people to a new residence or neighborhood. This section describes a Bring-a-Thing theme party, which is a variation of the

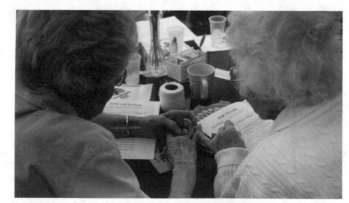

People enjoying themselves at a Bring-a-Thing Party

basic Bring-a-Thing activity. Appendix 1 provides materials you can duplicate and use for your Bring-a-Thing Party.

Planning a Bring-a-Thing Party

- Pencils will be needed, so have enough for the people you have invited.
- Have something for people to drink when they arrive. Coffee and juice will be refreshing, and will help put people at ease during the arrival period.
- Plan an easy dessert that can be served after the activity.

How to Publicize the Activity

The following sample notice or invitation may be mailed out or posted on a bulletin board.

YOU ARE INVITED TO A BRING-A-THING PARTY

Dessert Provided!

Simply *Bring-a-Thing* to the party—
bring some object you have saved because it connects you to
a meaningful experience or relationship. Be willing to tell a
story about it. The *thing* may be anything that has
significance to you—a stone, a picture, a gift.
It may be something you are wearing or something you
always carry with you. Any *thing* works!

At the party, you will be able to

- Use the object to get to know other people
- Tell your story
- Exchange experiences

DATE: _____

TIME: _____

PLACE: _____

How to Do the Activity

Following is a suggested plan for the activity:

	Minutes
• Arrive, enjoy punch, fill out name tags	14
• Form pairs	4
• Outline your story (on your Personal Story Record)	4
• Name your story (on your Personal Story Record)	4
• Partner #1 tells story	3
• Partner #2 tells story back	2
• Partner #2 tells story	3
• Partner #1 tells story back	2
• Tell stories to group	10
• Refreshments	<u>4</u>

Total: 50 minutes

~ Chapter 8 ~

Reminiscing in Various Care Settings

REMINISCING IS A STIMULATING ACTIVITY FOR SENIORS who live independently in their own homes, apartments, or condominiums. In all such settings reminiscing activities can be used successfully to help provide a way to meet their social needs through their own efforts. Should they wish to have additional support in order to maximize their sense of well-being, a continuum of support and healthcare services exists from which people may choose.

Long-term care[1] covers the entire range of elder care situations, from independent or residential living to congregate living, assisted living, nursing care, and hospital care—a continuum of healthcare. We identify possible opportunities for reminiscing in settings for independent living and residences visited by healthcare professionals, as well as in senior centers, daycare centers, assisted-living centers, nursing homes, and hospitals.

INDEPENDENT LIVING

IN BOTH RESIDENTIAL OR INDEPENDENT LIVING SETTINGS, the basic service package offered is housing. People move to and fro with ease and are actively engaged in the life of the community, partici-

---

[1] For more information on long-term care, contact the following trade associations:

(a) American Health Care Association (AHCA), 1201 L Street NW, Washington, DC 20005-4014, 202-842-4444

(b) American Association of Homes and Services for the Aging (AASHA), 901 E Street NW, Suite 500, Washington, DC 200004-2011, 202-508-9434

pating in volunteer activities and enjoying memberships in organizations. They enjoy reminiscing and reflecting with others on their life experiences. In the process of reminiscing about meaningful life experiences, current and new residents find common ground with one another. Consequently, new residents gain a sense of belonging and become integrated in the group, and current residents find ways to connect with and get to know new residents.

SENIOR CENTERS

SENIOR CENTERS PROVIDE ACTIVITIES for a wide variety of people who live on their own or who live independently in residential centers. Meals, bus trips, tax assistance, card clubs, and health screenings may all be part of the programming at a senior center.

Reminiscing activities can be used very effectively at senior centers. Bus tours, for example, provide excellent opportunities for conversing and reminiscing. Invite participants to notice things on a tour that they would be willing to tell about when they return. Provide pencils and small notebooks for people to record their thoughts to bring back later.

All kinds of activities at the senior center can offer opportunities for reminiscing. Ask people to share with others whose interests have been similar to theirs. Reminiscing will begin spontaneously.

An exciting example of this kind of setting is the Center for Active Generations in Sioux Falls, South Dakota. This new, attractive facility hosts a variety of activities including reminiscence that brings together people of all ages. Anyone visiting it will typically see elders engaged as teachers and participants in numerous activities, all of which provide opportunities for sharing stories.

Activities include:
- Senior services (hearing, vision, and blood pressure screens)
- Arts and crafts (rug weaving, ceramics, painting, embroidery, calligraphy)
- Card clubs (whist, bridge, cribbage, pinochle)
- Dances and dance classes (ballroom, line, square, tap)
- Drop-in activities (coffee shop, reminiscing, sing-alongs, bingo, potlucks, films)

- Fitness and wellness (weights, aerobics, walking, stretching)
- Lifelong learning (dress for less, safety and first aid, skin care, bird watching, healthy eating/cooking, travel, use of camcorders, doll collecting, arts, relaxation)
- Outdoor adventure (miniature golf, hiking, wildlife observation)
- Sports (pool, shuffleboard, biking, badminton, horseshoes)
- Special events (Halloween and other seasonal parties, hobby and craft parties, music programs)
- Trips and travel (lunch tours, fall foliage tours, local industry tours, local fire station tour, national and international charter tours)
- Volunteer activities (gift shop clerk, daybreak receptionist, Meals-on-Wheels packer, bingo caller, special-event coordinator, rug room volunteer, craft show volunteer, meal site host, serving and clean-up crew, craft instructor, holiday decorator, computer instructors, trip organizer)
- Computer classes (how to get started, learning to use the mouse, keyboarding, typing a letter, saving and printing your work)
- Intergenerational activities (dances, daycare).

HOME HELP AND HOME NURSES

IF SUPPORT IS REQUIRED to make it possible for people to remain at home, home helpers may be available. They visit during the week to help with cleaning and other chores, as well as to provide social interaction and opportunity for reminiscing one-on-one. Meals-on-Wheels is one support activity in this category. If additional skilled nursing help is required so someone can stay in his or her home, visiting public health nurses may be available to give injections, supervise medications, or provide therapy. Home visits provide ideal opportunities for reminiscing—both for the visitors and the person being visited.

DAYCARE CENTERS

PEOPLE WHO HAVE NEEDS greater than what is provided by senior centers may make use of daycare centers. In addition to providing care for seniors, these daycare centers also provide respite for family members or friends who may be providing extensive care. Some daycare centers provide transportation to and from the center. A hot meal is provided during the day. Crafts are often a focus at daycare centers, and they provide excellent opportunities for reminiscing activities.

At the Drabeck Day Center in Oslo, Norway, people work on crafts in small groups of three or four. While they are working, participants visit with one another. Depending on the project—painting, clay molding, reed weaving, or polishing stones—people may have stories about similar activities they have done in the past. Often the article being produced is intended to be a gift for a family member, so the activity may encourage reminiscing about relatives—who they are, where they are, and what they have done in their lives. As friendships develop, conversations extend into other enjoyable topics.

ASSISTED-LIVING CENTERS

ACCORDING TO THE AMERICAN HEALTH CARE ASSOCIATION,[2] assisted-living services are one of the fastest growing areas of support for elders. Assisted-living centers promote quality of life through managed housing. Whether the living space is an apartment or a simple room, people are encouraged to bring some of their own furniture and put their own pictures on the walls. Basic services include up to three meals per day, a call system, scheduled transportation, twenty-four-hour staffing, and personal care services. Assistance may be offered for daily chores such as laundry; reminders to take medications are given. Assisted-living centers provide excellent opportunities for reminiscing activities. Such opportunities help integrate aspects of a person's life prior to admission with life in the new setting. In such centers, opportunities for reminiscing usually abound as residents participate in optional activities.

---

2 The American Health Care Association's 1996 publication *Key Concepts of Assisted Living* is an excellent resource for assisted-living caregivers.

Borghild Loken, at the Arbor Assisted Living Center in Lodi, California, initiated a reminiscing group that met weekly. People were invited to talk about a special memento with a neighbor. The activity quickly became popular, growing from just a few participants to a group of twenty or so. Conversations begun during the reminiscing group spilled over to meal times and friendships flourished.

NURSING HOMES

PEOPLE WHO NEED CARE, BUT NOT HOSPITALIZATION, may live in nursing homes. When family members come to visit, they can be encouraged to bring items that are familiar to the resident. The objects serve as the basis for conversations as they bring to mind shared family experiences. Reminiscing is a good way to create meaningful interactions. Different objects can be brought each visit. The time together will be looked forward to by both the visitor and the resident.

HOSPITALS

IN THE EVENT THERE IS AN ACUTE NEED FOR MEDICAL CARE due to illness or injury, hospital services may be needed. Screening for such problems as senile dementia or Alzheimer's disease may initially be done in a hospital. Medical staff involved in treatment planning will want to meet with family members and others who are part of the patient's social network. The elder should be included in these discussions to the extent possible.

Reminiscing about familiar and enjoyable experiences can soothe some of the fears people may have when they are hospitalized. Pictures work well and are particularly suited to the hospital environment. Pictures are easily transported, they can be exchanged for new ones, and they can illustrate a variety of subjects. Snapshots work well and do not require much space.

~ Chapter 9 ~

Computers, Networks and Stories of Life Experiences

WHEN YOU LOOK AROUND TODAY, it may seem as if computers are taking over the world. Computers are on office desks, people's laps, kitchen tables, and living room floors. They are in homes, coffee shops, children's rooms, schools, and retirement centers.

One might ask if computers are just for typing letters, playing games, or keeping track of finances. Can computers, and the networks of wires that connect them, be helpful for people who would like to share stories of life experiences with others? The answer is an emphatic yes.

St. Olaf College student at the computer

Increasingly people of all ages are learning how to use computers to link with others on the Internet. The ease of connecting with others via computer is changing the way we think about our friends.

LINKING WITH FAMILY AND OLD FRIENDS

IT USED TO BE THAT WE WOULD LOSE CONTACT with friends who live far away. That no longer needs to be the case. Through the use of computers, we can swap stories about what we are doing now, as well as reminisce about things we used to do together. Such a continuing relationship with people who remember us from before has the potential to alter the way we think about ourselves now. It is amazing.

A person may read a story that has been posted on the Internet by a long-standing, but perhaps long-lost friend (someone from college, military outfit, hometown, scout troop, neighborhood, or church group). Because the reader senses a bond of common experiences, feelings, values, or ideas, he or she may be encouraged to send a message to the storyteller with the aim of renewing their friendship.

Frank Jamison wrote to us about reconnecting with friends.

"I have never been a letter writer until e-mail and the Internet. I can now actually stay connected to friends. It's a great idea. I've surfed the web and found links of all kinds."

Reading stories written on the Internet may facilitate the discovery of new friendships. The developing friendship will be based on a perception of common experiences, feelings, values, or ideas. While reading experiences others have posted, you may discover a person with a common interest in certain authors, an intellectual topic, gardening, movies, classic cars, or child development. As you write an e-mail directly to that person, you may find yourself beginning a new life-long friendship based on your common interest.

Jo Lowery lives in Minneapolis. Since retirement Jo has been using her home computer and modem to become active on the computer bulletin board scene. Listen to what Jo has to say about the use of computers.

"Computer projects are good for the soul. I see the computer as just another household appliance, like a food mixer, that helps me do what I want. Opportunities to be creative are important for all people but, in my experience, those opportunities narrow as we age. The computer opens all those opportunities up again. As I play with the computer, I try other things. There's even a close-up accessory that makes the print easier to read.

When I use the computer, I feel affirmed by the experience and I feel I am in a better position to do something else, to move on. When I am linked with someone over the computer, status differences are removed—particularly age differences. I think computer networks help break down barriers to cross-generational communication!"

HELPING ELDERS GET STARTED ON THE INTERNET

A short while ago we had a letter from an elder asking about using computers.

> "A few of the residents in our senior housing want to go on-line with the Internet; however, the logistics of money, time, and personnel are delaying, if not prohibiting, this from becoming a reality. How can we do this?"

Interestingly a few years ago the writer's comment would have been met with silence because computers in senior housing were a rare phenomenon indeed. But times are changing rapidly. This is the advice we might give today.

Place the Computer

We suggest you place a computer in your senior center on a trial basis. It does not have to be an overly expensive computer, a used one might do. Set it up on a counter where there is access to a phone line. It would be especially helpful if more than one person could sit in chairs in front of the computer at the same time. Learning to use the computer is often a team process.

Computers help build and maintain intergenerational relationships

Any local computer store can provide the equipment and information needed to connect a computer to an on-line network. A modem, a small box that connects the computer to the telephone line, will be installed. Then by typing a telephone number into the computer, you can make your connection to an on-line network.

Ask for Help

If you don't really know how to connect the computer to the modem and the modem to the phone line or you are a bit shy about trying out the system the first time by yourself, ask staff members if any of them have children who could be helpful. Or ask people you know if any of their grandchildren could give a hand. In this era of rapidly changing technology, it is often our children who are our teachers. As faculty members, we discovered this fact long ago, and we are now quite comfortable with this reality!

Take Small Steps

Organize demonstration programs such as the following:
- How to use the computer
- How to use a modem to get on-line
- How to access the many resources available on the World Wide Web

For best results, focus on one topic at a time so that those who participate do not become overwhelmed. Go slowly and make sure that people understand each step before going on to the next one.

Find Caring Teachers

Once again you may find young adults are the best teachers. It is important that these instructors are patient and that they enjoy working with elders. Young adults may need to slow down as they teach their elders these new skills. While e-mailing, storing files, and inserting photos have become second nature to our children, we often need a slower pace and hands-on practice when we are learning to use computers.

Ev Collins and Sandy Hager work together on Conversation Links

Start small

We recommend that you invite just a few elders to the demonstration programs in the beginning. First consider asking those who have expressed great interest in learning to use the computer. If some of those who attend the early sessions have a larger circle of friends, the word about the fun and excitement of gaining access to the Internet will spread rapidly.

Begin with Writing Stories of Experience

Ask each participant to write a short description of some life experience. Stories should be kept short; a few paragraphs will do just fine. Then the stories can be saved on individual disks. Participants can keep their disks and later return to the computer to add other stories whenever they want.

If you are thinking of setting up a computer for use by elders and others in your church, school, library, home, or coffee shop, use these suggestions and follow the advice of computer experts who are willing to help you set up your program.

SPECIAL WAYS TO MAKE CONNECTIONS ON THE INTERNET

THERE ARE A GROWING NUMBER OF WAYS you can use the Internet to chat on-line with others or to find information on topics such as health issues or foreign travel. One program that helps people share stories of life experiences with others on the Internet is called Conversation Links™. Since we have had a hand in the development of Conversation Links, we want to tell you about its potential.

Conversation Links— it's like talking across the back fence

Conversation Links has an important role to play any place people are using computers to access the Internet. *Conversation Links* helps people tell stories of their life experiences and connects people who have common interests. Possibilities for making connections are unlimited when these stories are being told on the Internet.

The back fence has a long tradition of calling up memories as a place where neighbors talked with one another. Actually talking to one another is an important part of what being a neighbor is all about! In reality, any informal place can serve as the back fence where we can tell our stories to one another—over coffee, during a meal, or while playing golf or bridge. *Conversation Links*, is just such a place; it is the new back fence.

Conversation Links provides a way to make contact with people throughout the U.S. and around the world. For less than the cost of phone calls, people with similar interests and

Conversation Links—
like talking across the back fence

experiences can share memories and ideas. Any number of people can be potential storytelling pals through this network.

Why Conversation Links *is Helpful*

Conversation Links is especially useful for people who have lost contact with those who shared experiences with them in the past. It is available to people who are sick, have difficulty getting around, don't have transportation, or have lost contact with old friends. It is accessible to people who have moved away from their homes, and it reestablishes contact even with people on the other side of the world. It enables people to contribute to the education of students of all ages around the globe.

Writing about your life not only serves the purpose of connecting you to old friends and opening up the possibility of new friendships, it may also help you feel good about yourself. Helen Nelson and Eric Jacobsen from the Fairlawn Good Samaritan Health Center in Gresham, Oregon, provide us with these insights on how helpful it can be to write down life experiences.

Helen said:

> "Telling stories about the past helps you to feel better and less lonely. It gives you pleasure and energy. I think it is better to tell stories about the good things that happened. That helps us feel good and seems to work on the body in some way. When experiences are pleasurable and we think about them, then we want to tell more stories. It raises our pleasure and energy when we write about the good times. We have more energy to go to meetings, play cards, and get out. That is what is important.
>
> Storytelling reduces depression and loneliness. We have all learned a great deal over our lifetime, and we can use those experiences now. Whether we have succeeded or failed at what we have tried, we have learned how to cope. The active people here are those who use the interests and talents they have learned over the years. They don't just sit around and wail about what went wrong in life, they talk about their good experiences and use their talents. When people have an outside interest to look forward to, this reduces depression and loneliness."

Eric added:

> "When I started writing, it was interesting to me to remember the things that I used to do. I began to wonder even more about the kind of life I had lived. I wondered what happened to my old playmates. It is interesting to think back on that—sometimes it is like a dream. I usually think about just the good memories and don't remember the other things so well. Now that I've written some of my stories down and I think about it, I had an interesting life. When I read other stories, I realize that mine sounds as interesting."

The Internet's advantage over the telephone is that a person can find and make connections easily and at a fraction of the cost of phone calls.

Leaving a Legacy

Conversation Links connections can be made between older and younger people through special projects sponsored by schools, libraries, senior centers, or Internet services such as the *Intercultural Email Classroom Connection* (www.iecc.org). This website is a free e-mail and Internet service that helps elders, teachers, students, and community groups find partners for educationally focused international and intergenerational conversations and projects.

IECC services enable elders to walk into virtual classrooms of students anywhere on the globe. The service has established three e-mail lists that enable elders to link with students.

IECC-InterGen enables persons who are 50-years old and older (50+ volunteers) to identify meaningful life experiences they would be willing to talk about with elementary, secondary, or higher education students.

IECC-GlobalGrandparents helps persons of grandparent-age link with classrooms of elementary-age students to engage in broad-ranging, enjoyable conversations.

IECC-ClassroomMentors enables volunteers of all ages to be helpful to students. Volunteers may, for example, be adult friends, serve as mentors, or assist with history, math, or science lessons.

Posting one's story on the Internet through *Conversation Links* provides a handy way to record stories that can be left as a legacy for families and friends.

Arch Leean, professor emeritus of art at St. Olaf College, points out how important this legacy is. He reminds us that listening to the messages of elders may give us insights into life.

"[Elders] have found answers to lots of life's questions, and we need to be able to hear them and pass them along."

Gen Lewis, director of a project called Yarns of Yesteryear at the University of Wisconsin Division of Outreach, made another important point in her letter to us.

"To children today, the lifestyles of fifty or more years ago are more alien than an episode from *Star Wars*! So much has changed so fast since the beginning of this century. We need to be sure the information is preserved for future generations."

Connection Possibilities

The Internet provides a unique way for people to reconnect with special friends they have lost contact with over the years. It is a way of keeping networks alive. It maintains bonds among old acquaintances.

Not only does the virtual community of the Internet allow on-line connections and socialization, but often those Internet links lead to wonderful face-to-face meetings that otherwise may never have happened.

A STORY SHARED

HERE IS A STORY WILLIS DROEGEMUELLER of the Remick Ridge Retirement Residence in Windom, Minnesota, posted on the Internet. Certainly thousands of families can relate to Willis' World War II experience.

"I have carried a picture in my billfold since Christmas 1944, fifty-some years. It shows my young son, Kenny, sitting on my knee. Both of us are dressed as sailors.

I went into the Navy two months after Pearl Harbor. At that time they took in people who had a trade. They started me out as an electrician's mate because of my background. I signed up for two years, but as soon as I got in, they changed the term to the duration of the war.

I went to boot camp for only three weeks, just long enough to get my shots at Great Lakes. Then I was sent to Glenview, Illinois, and later to the University of Minnesota to fill in a maintenance vacancy. I stayed there for ten months.

My wife, Doris, lived with me off the base. My son, Kenny, was born there. New orders arrived when he was about four months old. Doris and Kenny had to go back to Fairmont, where my folks lived; and I was transferred to Yorktown, Virginia, to mine-warfare school, and then went to sea in the Pacific.

I stayed there for two years, then got thirty days leave to go home at Christmas-time. I caught a ride back on a heavy cruiser that had been damaged by three torpedo hits in the Pacific. It took us three days to go from Panama to Norfolk. There was no place to sleep except on the deck on our seabags.

From Norfolk, I took the train to the Twin Cities. My dad picked me up and drove back to Fairmont. When I came in the back door of the house, Kenny was running around having fun. When he saw me, he just stopped and stared at me. My father asked him who I was. Kenny said, "That's my dad." My wife, Doris, had been showing him pictures of me while I was gone.

So we had a picture of both Kenny and me in sailor suits. That is why I have kept this in my billfold for over fifty years."

POSSIBLE STORY TOPICS

BELOW ARE POSSIBLE TOPICS THAT MAY REMIND YOU of experiences you could relate on the Internet. Of course, if this list also brings to mind a story you want to tell a person sitting next to you or someone you can reach on the telephone, so much the better!

Willis Droegemueller holding a picture of his son and himself

Adventure stories
Airplane stories
Animal and
  pet stories
Baby stories
Book stories
Building something
  stories
Car stories
Cartoon favorites
Celebrity stories
Child-raising stories
Childhood stories
Christmas stories
Church stories
Circus stories
City stories
Courage stories
Close-call stories

Cold War stories
College/University
  stories
Coming home
  stories
Cooking/food
  stories
Courtship stories
Cowboy/ranch
  stories
Daughter stories
Decision-making
  stories
Depression Era
  stories
Dieting stories
Difficulty stories
Disappointment
  stories
Doll stories

Dream stories
Easter stories
Electrical failure
  stories
Entrepreneurial
  stories
Escape stories
Faith stories
Family stories
Farm stories
Father-Child stories
Fire stories
Fishing/hunting
  stories
Funny stories
Game stories
Gardening stories
Gift stories
Grandmother stories

Grandfather stories
Grandchild stories
Halloween stories
Happily-ever-after stories
Happy stories
Hard times stories
Hard work stories
Hiking/camping stories
History stories
Hobby stories
Hometown stories
Honeymoon stories
Immigration stories
Job-related stories
Joy stories
Korean War stories
Leadership stories
Library stories
Living abroad stories
Lost-and -found stories
Marooned stories
Marriage stories
Military stories
Miracle stories

Mother/child stories
Movie stories
Moving stories
Music stories
Mystery stories
Nature stories
Neighbor stories
Ocean stories
Picnic stories
Plumbing stories
Police stories
Prank stories
Prom stories
Radio stories
Recipe stories
Recovery stories
Relationship stories
Religious stories
Retirement stories
Reunion stories
Ritual stories
Romance stories
Sailing stories
School stories
Shopping stories
Son stories
Sports/athletics stories

Standing firm stories
Storm stories
Sunday School stories
Survival stories
Teaching stories
Thanksgiving stories
Theater stories
Toy stories
Tool stories
Train stories
Travel stories
Tree house stories
Trespassing stories
TV stories
UFO stories
Vacation stories
Vietnam protest stories
Vietnam War stories
World War II stories
Zoo stories

~ *Chapter 10* ~

Special Audiences

HELPING OUR HEARING IMPROVES REMEMBERING because we can't remember what we have never heard! According to the National Center for Health Statistics, hearing loss affects more than 50% of men and 30% of women over sixty-five years of age. As hearing difficulties increase, people may experience greater difficulty trying to converse. Their ability to reminisce may be threatened unless they receive help.

Eleanor Devine is a writer, wife, mother and member of the North Shore Senior Center in Winnetka, Illinois. She says,

> "Losing hearing means losing the beauty of voices and music, the patter of small children, the small tones of love. But worst of all, it means not knowing what is going on—feeling left out. Hard-of-hearing people have to work three times harder on a train, at a party, at a street corner, on the telephone, or at their desks to get the story, to keep track of people, to catch up on the news, or to be sure of instructions."[1]

In this section, we will consider how hearing can hinder reminiscing about thoughts, feelings, and experiences. We will also look at ways to increase the likelihood people can hear one another.

RECOGNIZING HEARING DIFFICULTIES

We are often unaware of people around us who have hearing disabilities. Visual disabilities are easier for us to notice because many people wear glasses to alleviate this difficulty. We don't think it is unusual when someone needs glasses; in fact, we consider glasses to be normal and necessary. Hearing aids are less common and less

---

[1] (*Shhh*, March/April, 1987, p. 7)

noticeable than glasses, but just as necessary. Glasses and hearing aids are both tools—helpers for our seeing and helpers for our hearing.

It may be difficult to notice when a person is losing hearing sensitivity because changes in hearing sensitivity can occur gradually. Even the person who is experiencing the change in hearing may not be aware of the loss because it is occurring so gradually.

The first clue to a hearing loss may be difficulty in hearing exactly what people are saying. Voices may sound muffled.

Loraine DiPietro is director of the National Information Center on Deafness, and she is also hearing impaired. She told us,

> "When I meet new people, I sometimes have trouble hearing their names and may use various coping strategies such as asking them to spell the name. Sometimes the strategies fail. The end result is that when I meet these people in the future, I may clearly remember them—their faces, our conversation, and even where I met them—but I don't remember their names."

HOW TO HELP PEOPLE REMINISCE WHO HAVE HEARING LOSS

SOMETIMES IT IS DIFFICULT FOR THE PERSON who is hearing-impaired to recognize that a hearing loss has occurred, so it is no wonder the hearing loss is difficult for friends to recognize. It is important that people acknowledge they are having difficulty hearing. Then friends can respond by speaking louder or more directly.

Remove Background Noise

The setting influences a person's ability to hear. Anyone would have difficulty hearing inside a factory with noisy machines pounding up and down. How much hearing disability exists depends upon how much background noise there is.

Most people with hearing difficulties have more trouble understanding speech when there is background noise. Background noise masks, or covers up, the sound. Background noise can even wipe out speech completely; some people just don't hear anything at all until things are quieter. Running water is a difficult background noise, as are the sounds of ventilation fans or blowers, rustling newspapers, or crowds of people. Background noise should be stopped whenever possible.

Coping with Noise when it Can't Be Removed

The noisiest places are rooms with shiny surfaces. Enameled walls, linoleum floors, and polished ceilings are designed to be easy to clean; however, everyone seems to be shouting in such a room. When the room is filled with people talking enthusiastically and moving about, all the noises blend together and create confusion. Adding a curtain or overstuffed chairs to the room will help absorb the noise and make individual sounds more easily distinguishable.

Encourage people to improve their ability to hear by moving away from the noise source. When there is a lot of talking and chattering in the room, suggest that people go to a part of the room where there is less noise. The following information will help people with hearing disabilities find those quieter spots.

- Curtains absorb the sound, rather than reflect it. It is easier for people to hear if they stand by a curtain, rather than in the middle of the room.
- A person can sit down on a couch to talk with a friend because sounds will be absorbed by that couch, instead of being reflected toward the listener.
- Find a couch next to a drape or some kind of absorbent material. That will be the quietest place to converse.

Encourage people to pick a quiet spot when they want to have conversations. As a health professional, family member, or other friend, you can encourage people to find ways to cope with the background noise that decreases their ability to hear. Being able to hear better will mean that reminiscing is more fun. When people hear better, their chances of remembering are improved. If something prevents them from hearing, reminiscing with others is more difficult.

OTHER SPECIAL AUDIENCES

REMINISCING ACTIVITIES CAN BE ADAPTED for use with other special audiences such as for those suffering vision loss. You can invite participants to make mental images of an object or an experience or invite them to describe experiences using the language of the senses, such as smell and touch. The power of imagery is great, regardless of what sense is involved.

~ Chapter 11 ~

How to Conduct An In-Service Training On Reminiscence

THIS SECTION DESCRIBES HOW TO INTEREST activity leaders in planning reminiscing activities. If you know leaders who have been looking for meaningful ways to engage people, share how you are using reminiscing activities in your own work. Use whatever approaches you think will help them become familiar with reminiscing.

Perhaps you feel that reminiscing activities could be meaningful for people in your organization or group. The in-service training presented in this chapter can be used to introduce people to the process involved in reminiscing.

The Process   45 minutes

1. Introduce your presentation. Pass out copies of this book.
2. Summarize the research results on the connection between reminiscing and social support. Use the graphs at the end of this chapter to show how a person's sense of esteem decreases as the person ages.

    Figure 1: Social support begins to decrease at age twenty. Retired people have significantly fewer opportunities for social support than younger people do.

    Figure 2: Men and women differ in the amount of mutual support they feel they receive. Men of retirement age feel they are no longer esteemed by others.

    Figure 3: As people grow older, they feel they have fewer opportunities to talk about their interests.

3. Do a reminiscence activity such as Bring-A-Thing, following the steps suggested in this book. This activity helps people develop many of the skills that research shows are important in helping people remain actively engaged with others.

After the Process

1. Explain to the participants that the activity they just experienced came from this book. Explain that it is one of the activities based on the research mentioned at the beginning of the book that has been used internationally with diverse audiences.

2. To help people generate ideas for using reminiscing in their interactions with others, ask them to take a few minutes at this time to skim through the table of contents of this book. Ask them to mark parts of interest to them, given their own experiences. Mention that in a few minutes you will ask them to share what they marked with a partner. Pairs will then be asked to share what they talked about with the larger group.

3. Invite participants to take their copies of this book home. Ask them to prepare for a future meeting by rereading sections they marked in the book. Suggest that they come to the next meeting prepared to share their ideas.

4. Ask people to think about ways they could use the activities in this book in their own work. Encourage them to try out the activities. Ask them to keep notes on how they used the activities, their observations about how the activities worked, and suggestions for what they want to repeat in the future.

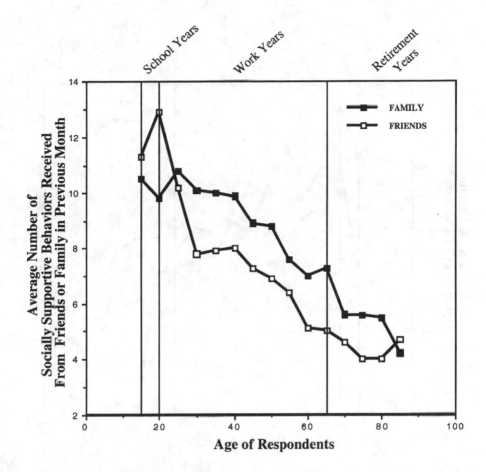

Fig. 1. Opportunities to give and receive social support from family and friends are fewer as we grow older.
(This analysis is based on responses from 1457 females and 740 males.)

From: Thorsheim, H. & Roberts, B. (1990). Empowerment through storysharing: Communication and reciprocal social support among older persons. In H. Giles, N. Coupland, and J. Wiemann (Eds.). *Communication, Health and the Elderly.* Fulbright Colloquium Series No. 8, (pp. 114-125). London: Manchester University Press.

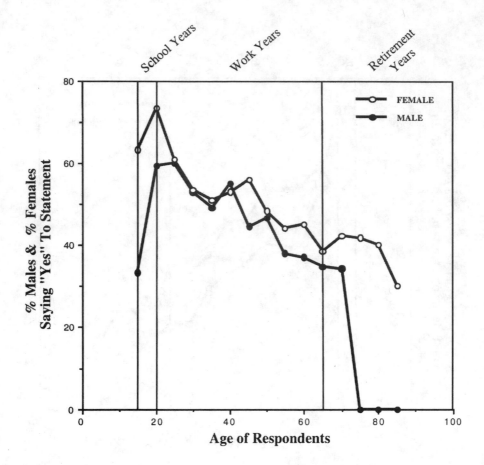

Fig. 2. Opportunities to receive esteem from others are fewer as we grow older, especially for men after retirement.
People were asked if they agreed (Yes) or disagreed (No) with the statement "Friends express esteem or respect for a competency or personal quality of mine." (This analysis is based on responses from 1457 females and 740 males.)

From Thorsheim, H., & Roberts, B. (1992). *How to empower persons by helping them tell their story.* Paper presented at the 38th Annual Meetings of the American Society on Aging, San Diego, CA.

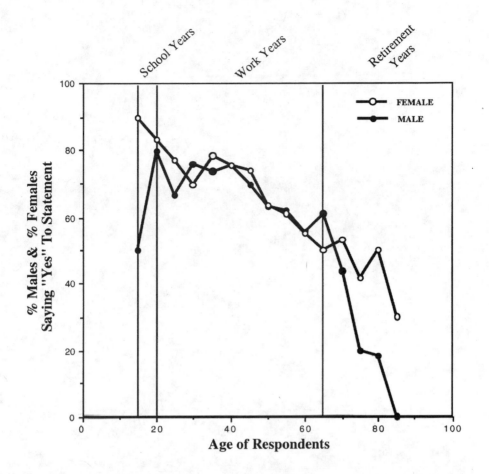

Fig. 3. Opportunities to talk about our interests are fewer as we grow older.

People were asked if they agreed (Yes) or disagreed (No) with the statement "Friends talk with me about some interest of mine." (This analysis is based on responses from 1457 females and 740 males.)

From Thorsheim, H., & Roberts, B. (1992). *How to empower persons by helping them tell their story.* Paper presented at the 38th Annual Meetings of the American Society on Aging, San Diego, CA.

~ *Glossary* ~

Anecdotes—Short narratives or stories told or written about meaningful events in one's life.

Collections—Objects saved because they fit some theme that is of interest or other importance.

Community—A group in which people are involved, feel a sense of belonging, can call one another by name, care what happens to one another, have the skills to link up with one another to give and receive support, and ask one another to be of assistance.

Conversation—To talk together socially, either in speech or in writing (as in letters or e-mail).

Empowerment—A sense of personal control over the things that matter to oneself. A sense of well-being or purpose. A sense of being appreciated and affirmed with dignity.

Engagement—To have one's interest and attention focused on an activity.

Engagement in Community—A four-part process in which people (1) name and are named by others, (2) care about others, (3) know how to link up with others to give and receive social support, and (4) are asked to help.

Haptic Memory—Memory for how things feel when we touch them; memory of characteristics such as texture or shape.

Heirloom—Special object that has existed in the family and may be passed along from parent to child.

IECC—Intercultural Email Classroom Connections is a means for connecting students in classrooms with other students or elders.

Internet—The world-wide electronic communication network that enables people to use computers to have conversations with others anywhere around the globe.

Life Story—Description of life experiences, oral or written, about events across the life of a person, group of people, or organization.

Links—Bonds or ties connecting people in personally meaningful ways.

Mementos—Objects saved because they serve as reminders of prior experiences or events, often with good feelings attached.

Memory—The mental capacity and process by which we recall previous experiences, events, impressions, and relationships.

Mutual Reminiscing—A reciprocal process in which people share their stories, as well as actively listen while their partners tell their stories.

Networks—The links among people, such as those created when people are engaged in conversations

Pump-Primers—Techniques that help people remember experiences they like to think about and enjoy talking about.

Reminiscing—Telling stories, in an informal setting, about life experiences that are meaningful to the teller and about which he or she would like to tell.

Social Network—Informal relationships that have mutual significance (for good or bad). These relationships may develop between relatives, friends, neighbors, and co-workers.

Social Support—Informal help, in the form of words and deeds, that enables us feel to good about ourselves and others; a sense of fellowship. Social support is a two-way street with benefits of reduced stress and improved mental health for all people involved in the relationship.

Souvenir—Object that connects its owner to a special event, place, or experience.

Storytelling—People tell what is on their minds, what is important to them, and what they care about. The focus may be on current daily events or on events from the past.

Things/Objects—Items people have saved for a reason. They connect the owner with meaningful experiences and relationships and serve as pump-primers that help people tell their stories.

Well-being—A satisfying feeling generally characterized by a sense of connection to and belonging with others, of feeling competent, and of appreciating one's ability to make contributions that are meaningful in the lives of others.

~ References ~

Guide to Reminiscing Resources

It is helpful to have information at your fingertips that you can use to learn more about reminiscing-related topics. The following references have served as resources for the writing of this book. These references can provide you with background informa- tion on reminiscing, sharing personal life stories, and other related topics. Resourc- es are grouped in alphabetical order by topic. Each resource has a brief note about its focus.

Librarians enjoying new reminiscing resources
[Barbara Johnson and Joanne Kaye of the
Public Library in Northfield, Minnesota]

COMMUNICATION, EMPOWERMENT, AND REMINISCING

To FEEL EMPOWERED IS TO HAVE A SENSE OF WELL-BEING and a sense that your life has important meaning. These are the goals of the reminiscing activities in this book. Empowered people have a good sense of identity and some control over things that matter to them personally. They care about others; they feel that they belong and are accepted. They are asked to help in important ways and are appreci- ated for who they are and what they can do. The following resources

127

provide useful information about empowerment and its benefits.

American Association of Retired Persons. Reminiscence: *Finding Meaning in Memories*. Washington, DC: AARP

This wonderful resource for training reminiscing volunteers comes in a three-ring binder with slides, audio tape, and suggestions for volunteers. For information, contact AARP (202-434-2263).

Lloyd, P. (1991). The empowerment of elderly people. *Journal of Aging Studies*, 5(2), 125-135.

Empowerment has been one of the guiding principles in our research and writing. This article is a useful one for reflecting on empowerment in the case of older persons.

Maslow, A. (1970). *Motivation and Personality*. (2nd ed.). New York: Harper and Row.

This work is a classic introduction to the thinking of this great psychologist on a hierarchy of human needs. The hierarchy culminates in self-actualization.

Rappaport, J. (1990). Research methods and the empowerment social agenda. In P. Tolan, C. Keys, F. Chertok, & L. Jason (Eds.), *Researching Community Psychology: Issues of Theory and Methods* (pp. 51-63). Washington, DC.: American Psychological Association.

Rappaport and his colleagues at the University of Illinois are among the first to research the concept of empowerment. This article provides insights on the potential of empowerment for social change.

Roberts, B., & Thorsheim, H. (1987). *Empowering Leadership*. Northfield, MN: St. Olaf College.

This book describes specific micro-empowering skills that research has shown to be at the heart of empowering styles of leadership. Any person in a leadership position, including healthcare workers, family members, and friends working with elder persons, can put these skills to use immediately.

Thorsheim, H., & Roberts, B. (1990). Empowerment through reminiscing: Communication and reciprocal social support among elders. In H. Giles, N. Coupland, & J. Wiemann (Eds.), *Fulbright Colloquium Series: No. 8. Communication, Health and the Elderly* (pp.

114-125). Manchester, England: University of Manchester.

The chapter describes reminiscing as a process in which people name things and people they care about and link up with others who have similar stories. The new friends develop mutual support networks that extend beyond the reminiscing activity. Reminiscing is described as an empowering process in which people invest in their own community by sharing their stories with one another.

Thorsheim, H., & Roberts, B. (1996). Praxis through shared lifestories: A design process for community empowerment through social elaboration of learning. In W. W. Gasparski, M. K. Mlicki, & B. B. Banathy (Eds.), *International Annual of Practical Philosophy and Methodology. Social Agency: Dilemmas and Education Praxiology* (pp. 233-250). New Brunswik, NJ: Transactions Publications, Rutgers University.

This chapter describes the importance of shared life stories in two community settings: (1) within the inner-city, among women in poverty and (2) across the life-span. A theoretical model is provided, showing how shared life stories build community by helping people know themselves, and others, better.

CROSS-CULTURAL PERSPECTIVES ON REMINISCING

REMINISCING AND STORYTELLING have a long and rich history in cultures around the world. Reminiscing can be used internationally as tools for working with elders. Many of the following resources illustrate cross-cultural studies being done by our colleagues in Norway. Other sources review issues to consider when using reminiscing with people from other cultures.

Bjelland, A. K., Danielsen, K., Helset, A., & Thorsen, K. (1992). Livsløp og livshistorier [Life course and life stories]. *Norwegian Gerontological Institute Report 4-1992*. Oslo, Norway.

This reference, written in Norwegian, is included to document the strong international research focus on the role of life stories in the lives of elders.

Howard, G. S. (1991). Culture Tales: A Narrative Approach to Thinking, Cross-cultural Psychology, and Psychotherapy. *American Psychologist,* March, 187-197.

Building bridges between cultures through sharing of stories of life experiences is a thrust of this article.

Ingebretsen, R. (1989). Mine, dine og våre erfaringer: Samtalegrupper for pårørende til aldersdemente [My, your, and our experiences: Conversation groups for family members of patients with senile dementia]. *Norwegian Gerontological Institute Report 6-1989.* Oslo, Norway.

This article, written in Norwegian, describes the use of reminiscence as a therapeutic tool for families.

Jebens, A. (1990). *Fra tradisjonelle Ledete Grupper til Selvtreningsgrupper* [From traditionally-led groups to self-training groups]. (The Network Project). Oslo, Norway: Diakonhjemmets Sykehus.

This article, written in Norwegian, describes the Heart Group, a remarkable support group for retired men recovering from heart bypass surgery. Physical therapy sessions in a swimming pool foster talking about life experiences.

Kleiner, R. J., & Okeke, B. I. (1991). Advances in Field Theory: New Approaches and Methods in Cross-cultural Research. *Journal of Cross-Cultural Psychology,* 22(4), 509-524.

This article points out issues to consider when working with cultures different from one's own. Though directed at researchers, the lessons apply just as well to applied settings.

Rø, O. C., Hendriksen, C., Kivela, S., & Thorslund, M. (1987). Intervention Studies among elderly people. *Scandinavian Journal of Primary Health Care,* 5, 163-168.

This article provides information that must be considered when designing interventions with elder persons. It also shares experiences from four Nordic countries.

Rosenwald, G. C., & Ochberg, R. L. (1992). *Storied lives: The Cultural Politics of Self-Understanding.* New Haven, NJ: Yale University.

This book explains how our stories are understood by each of us within the frame provided by our culture. Life stories are not only told about our lives but, in fact, are part of our lives, a kind of "organization of our experience," to use the words of the authors.

ELDERS' WISDOM AS RESOURCE

ELDERS ARE A RESERVOIR OF WISDOM FROM THEIR LIFE experiences; unfortunately for the elders themselves and for the rest of society, this reservoir of wisdom is not drawn on as it should be. These resources provide useful information about the nature of elder wisdom, the importance of encouraging elders to share their wisdom, and the possibilities of sharing this resource with people of all ages.

Baltes, P. B., & Smith, J. (1990). Toward a psychology of wisdom and its ontogenesis. In R. J. Sternberg (Ed.) *Wisdom: Its Nature, Origins and Development.* (pp. 87-120). New York: Cambridge University.

This chapter is related to the topic of wisdom. It describes how aging may include incorporating feelings into the thought process in a kind of practical intelligence.

Beverfelt, E. (1984). Old People Remember: A Contribution to Society. *Educational Gerontology,* 10, 233-244.

Beverfelt says, "The responsibility as culture-bearers is a challenge to old people. To enable them to participate and to use their experience is a challenge to society." The article describes a positive project that encouraged two thousand elders to share their stories. This is a valuable resource for national and regional history.

Dittman-Kohli, F., & Baltes, P. B. (1990). Toward a neofunctionalist conception of adult intellectual development: Wisdom as a prototypical case of intellectual growth. In C. Alexander & E. Langer (Eds.), *Higher Stages of Human Development* (pp. 54-78). New York: Oxford University.

The chapter describes how wisdom grows when a person has learned to deal practically with complex, everyday life tasks.

Hagestad, G. (1987). Able elderly in the family context: Changes, chances, and challenges. *Gerontologist,* 27(4), 417-422.

Aged persons are viewed not as a problem, but as a resource. This article makes the case that older people and their memories and stories of experiences are rich, but under-utilized, resources for themselves and for society. Hagestad states, "Older family members can help the young build bridges to the past, and the young can help make a rapidly changing culture and technology more understandable."

Hopewell, J. F. (1987). Storytelling. In *Congregations: Stories and structures* (pp. 140-149). Philadelphia: Fortress.

Church congregational activities provide ample and rich opportunities for talking about what is going on in one's life, that is, to tell one's stories. This book is tailored specifically to those who wish to build on this rich resource for their community.

Staude, J. (1981). *Wisdom and Age: The Adventures of Later Life.* Berkeley, CA: Ross.

This book discusses the wisdom of experience, aging and development, and creativity and community.

Sternberg, R. (1990). *Wisdom: Its Nature, Origins and Development.* Cambridge, MA: Cambridge University.

"Wisdom is the stories of our lives," someone once told us, "because our stories pull our experiences together with what we think and feel about them." This book contains thoughtful discussion about the concept of wisdom and our understanding of wisdom through the ages.

Thorsheim, H., & Roberts, B. (1990c). *Elders as Consultants: The Lifestories Program.* [Video].

This film presents the plan, process, and summary of the Elders as Consultants program, a project developed in rural communities, funded by the Blandin Foundation. This video won an honorable mention in the National Media Owl Awards sponsored by the Retirement Research Foundation.

INTERVENTION PRINCIPLES

DR. JAMES KELLY'S SUGGESTIONS in the following resources can help to make any kind of psycho-social intervention a success. These resources have served as helpful guides as we developed and tested the activities found in this book.

Kelly, J. (1986). An ecological paradigm: Defining mental health as a preventive service. In J. G. Kelly & R. E. Hess (Eds.), *Prevention in human services: The ecology of prevention: Illustrating Mental Health Consultation* (pp. 1-36). New York: Haworth.

Ten principles for creative, thoughtful mental health interventions are explained in this readable article.

Kelly, J. (1988). *Guide to Conducting Prevention Research in Communities.* New York: Haworth.

This book describes several ways development of a sense of community fosters psycho-social health.

LIFE REVIEW

DR. ROBERT BUTLER'S "STRUCTURED LIFE REVIEW" was the first planned approach to using reminiscence as a tool for helping elders. Dr. Butler pioneered work in reminiscing and telling life stories as a way to empower people. He has dedicated his professional life to promoting the dignity of elder persons. These resources contain the reference for Butler's foundational presentation of "Life Review," as well as other perspectives on the helpfulness of the approach.

Butler, R. (1968). The life review: An interpretation of reminiscence in the aged. In B. L. Neugarten (Ed.) *Middle Age and Aging,* (pp. 486-494). Chicago: University of Chicago. (Original work published in 1963).

This was the ground-breaking article that introduced the use of life review, reminiscence, and personal narrative as important for elders' sense of meaning and dignity. It would be worthwhile for anyone entering the field of reminiscing to read this informative and historic chapter.

Conway, M. A. (1990). *Autobiographical Memory.* Philadelphia: Open University.

The book is a useful reference on memory for one's own personal life history. Topics such as vivid flashbulb memories, emotions and the sense of self, and remembering the past as a process of retrieval are included.

Foss, L. (1991). Minnearbeid med eldre i grupper: Jeg er også den jeg var. [Memory work with elders in groups: "I am also the person I was"]. *Sosionomen,* 16, 2-7.

This article, published in Norwegian, makes the point that elders' sense of who they are is connected with who they have always seen themselves to be, as well as who they have developed into over the years.

Haight, B. K., & Olson, M. (1989). Teaching home health aides the use of life review. *Journal of Nursing Staff Development,* January/February, 110-116.

Life review, a particular structured approach to reminiscing, was first developed by Robert Butler. This article describes ways to make this approach available for use by home health aides.

Meyerhoff, B. (1992). *Remembered Lives: The Work of Ritual, Storytelling, and Growing Older.* Ann Arbor, MI: University of Michigan.

In this sensitively written book, the author speaks of "re-membered" lives—lives put back together through reflecting autobiographically on one's own life history.

Myerhoff, B. (1982). Life history among the elderly: Performance, visibility, and remembering. In Jay Ruby (Ed.), *A Crack in the Mirror: Reflexive Perspectives in Anthropology* (pp. 99-117). Philadelphia: University of Philadelphia.

Telling one's life history is described as a way for persons to become visible. The author makes the case that telling one's life history is an essential activity for psychological health as we grow older.

Reason, P., & Hawkins, P. (1988). Storytelling as inquiry. In P. Reason (Ed.), *Human Inquiry in Action: Developments in New Paradigm Research* (pp. 79-101). London: Sage.

Experience is viewed as being at the root of one's stories. Stories may describe those experiences and explain their meaning.

MEANING OF OBJECTS

WE SAVE OBJECTS BECAUSE THEY CONNECT US with meaningful experiences and relationships. The following resources provide insights about objects and their meaning and describe how the objects serve as stimuli that help connect the past to the present.

Burnside, I. (1994). Using props in reminiscence groups. In B. Haight & J. Webster (Eds.), *The Art and Science of Reminiscing: Theory, Research, Methods, and Applications* (pp. 151-163). London: Taylor and Francis.

An expert in research on reminiscing, author Irene Burnside presents research findings on the role *things* can play in reminiscence groups.

Csikszentmihalyi, M., & Rochberg-Halton, E. (1981). *The Meaning of Things: Domestic Symbols and the Self.* New York: Cambridge University.

This book documents the power of ordinary objects in life to evoke meaningful memories of life experiences.

Radley, A. (1990). Artifacts, memory and a sense of the past. In D. Middleton & D. Edwards (Eds.), *Collective Remembering* (pp. 46-59). London: Sage.

The author develops the idea that objects are "concrete instances of past events," the meaning of which is presented in story. Read this article, along with the articles by Burnside, Csikszentmihalyi and Rochberg-Halton, and Thorsheim and Roberts (1995), for a firm base on the role of things as stimulants for reminiscing.

ORAL HISTORY

WHEN PEOPLE REMINISCE, THEIR STORIES often contain vital information about the cultural history of a place, an organization, or a family. To record the story as it is being told, in the language of the telling, is to record oral history.

Hoopes, J. (1979). *Oral History*. Chapel Hill, NC: University of North Carolina.

The book defines oral history as an individual's spoken memories of his or her life, people known, and events witnessed or participated in. It provides helpful steps for planning an oral history interview, carrying it out, and transcribing the stories. This book is one of the best resources in oral history.

REMINISCING AND HEALTH

REMINISCING IS GOOD FOR HEALTH and for a sense of well-being. These resources provide information about the key role communication, reminiscing, and storytelling have in maintaining good health.

Becker, G., & Kaufman, S. (1988). Old age, rehabilitation and research: A review of the issues. *Gerontologist,* 28(4), 459-468.

This article is a good background summary of a number of issues related to aging and health.

Birren, J. E., & Deutchman, D. E. (1991). *Guiding Autobiography Groups for Older Adults: Exploring the Fabric of Life.* Baltimore: Johns Hopkins University.

This 146-page book includes sections titled "Strengthening the Fabric of Life," "Leading a Guided Autobiography Group," "The Healing Power of the Group," "The Importance of Guiding Themes," "Encouraging Creativity and Divergent Thinking," "Mastering Potential Obstacles in the Group Process," "The Next Steps after Guided Autobiography," "A Professional's Guide to the Literature," and "Implications for Future Research."

Fiedler, J., Thorsheim, H., & Roberts, B. (1998). Cardiac Concomitants of Reminiscing. Paper presented at the Second International Conference on Psychophysiology in Ergonomics, Osaka, Japan, October 7-8.

In this preliminary study, we found evidence that strongly suggested systolic blood pressure and heart rate are lowered significantly below resting baseline levels when people *listen* to meaningful reminiscing. In contrast, when people listen to stories or to information that is not meaningful to them, there is no similar lowering of blood pressure and heart rate. We view our findings about the benefits for blood pressure and heart rate to be preliminary results that need to be examined in future studies.

Kreps, G. (1989). Communication and health. In E. B. Ray & L. Donohew (Eds.), *Communication in Health Care Contexts: A Systems Perspective* (pp. 187-203). Hillsdale, NJ: Erlbaum.

This article discusses the relationship between satisfactory levels of communication and one's health.

Sheridan, C. (1991). *Reminiscence: Uncovering a Lifetime of Memories.* Forest Knolls, CA: Elder Books.

Reminiscing is one of the most powerful healing activities for people affected by Alzheimer's disease. Through reviewing the past, people with Alzheimer's can see their contributions to life and experience positive feelings about themselves. The book will help families, friends, volunteers and, in fact, everyone who comes into repeated contact with a memory-impaired person, to develop reminiscing skills.

Thorsheim, H., and Roberts, B. (1990). *Reminiscing Together: Ways to Help us Keep Mentally Fit as We Grow Older.* Minneapolis, MN: CompCare Publishers.

This book contains memory-strengthening exercises that can easily be used as one goes about his or her daily work. It has ideas for helping memory-impaired clients/residents to remember who they are and to do so with a sense of respect and dignity. This book introduces reminiscing; provides a brief, but sound, introduction to how memory works; discusses the role of the senses of sight, hearing, smell, and touch; provides pump-primers for strengthening memory; suggests action ideas for volunteers; and provides an introduction to the AARP Reminiscence Program.

REMINISCING AS CONVERSATION

IT COULD BE SAID WITHOUT EXAGGERATION that every moment people converse with others, they are "telling stories," often stories that draw on their own life experiences. In short, they are reminiscing. These resources provide additional insights into reminiscing as conversation.

Danielsen, K. (1990). *De gammeldagse piker: eldre kvinner forteller om sitt liv.* [Girls of olden times: Elder women tell about their lives]. Oslo, Norway: Pax Forlag.

This short book, written in Norwegian, provides keen insights into how life stories are created through dialog either with oneself or with another person.

Heap, K. (1990). *Samtalen i eldreomsorgen: Kommunikasjon, minner, kriser, sorg* [Conversations in elder care: Communication, memories, crises, and concerns]. Oslo, Norway: Kommuneforlaget.

This book, written in Norwegian, describes the key role for health and well-being played by informal conversations with elders.

Middleton, D., & Edwards, D. (1990). *Collective Remembering*. London: Sage.

The edited chapters in this book discuss how conversational remembering is a way of retaining, as well as recovering, our own community's unique cultural history.

Polyani, L. (1989). *Telling the American Story: A Sructural and Cultural Analysis of Conversational Storytelling*. Cambridge, MA: MIT.

This book describes the cultural and social influences on the stories we tell and ways those stories recount and restructure our experiences.

Wertsch, J. V. (1985). *Vygotsky and the Social Formation of Mind*. Cambridge, MA: Harvard University.

This book describes the theoretical work of Vygotsky, who, in the 1920s, wrote about how people's thinking about their own experiences is enhanced by listening to other's reflections on their experiences.

White, W. R. (1982). *Speaking in Stories*. Minneapolis, MN: Augsburg.

Written originally for use in church communities, the book has helpful thoughts about the role of life stories in any community.

REMINISCING AND STORYTELLING THEORY

REMINISCING, STORYTELLING, AND PERSONAL NARRATIVE are hot topics in many professions. These resources are a sampling of storytelling theory.

Bruner, J. (1990). Autobiography and self. In J. Bruner, *Acts of meaning* (pp. 99-138). Cambridge, MA: Harvard University.

How humans extract meaning from their life experiences through autobiography and other forms of narrative is the focus of this chapter.

Coles, R. (1989). *The Call of Stories: Teaching and the Moral Imagination*. Boston: Houghton-Mifflin.

A quote from this book captures its flavor: "The people ... bring us their stories... We have to remember that what we hear is their story."

Haight, B., & Webster, J. (Eds.) (1994). *The Art and Science of Reminiscing: Theory, Research, Methods, and Applications.* London: Taylor and Francis.

This is a useful resource book, an asset in the library of anyone working with reminiscing, in any context.

Kovach, C. R. (1991). Reminiscence behavior: An empirical exploration. *Journal of Gerontological Nursing,* 17(12), 23-28.

This research article is useful in exploring the dimensions of reminiscing behavior.

Kovach, C. R. (1991). Reminiscence: Exploring the origins, processes, and consequences. *Nursing Forum,* 26(3), 14-20.

This article takes up where the previous article leaves off and delves into the activity of reminiscing.

Mandler, J. M. (1984). *Stories, Scripts, and Scenes.* Hillsdale, NJ: Erlbaum.

This is one of the first books to describe the relationship between story, or narrative, and ways of thinking.

McAdams, D. (1988). *Power, Intimacy, and the Life Story.* New York: Guilford.

The author begins his preface by quoting Joan Didion: "We tell ourselves stories in order to live." This book is about those kinds of stories.

Merriam, S. B. (1989). The structure of simple reminiscence. *Gerontologist,* 29(6), 761-767.

The article describes four stages in simple reminiscence: (1) Selection of a topic, following a pump-primer activity; (2) immersion, in which the reminiscer may feel transported to the scene; (3) withdrawal, where the reminiscer gradually distances him or herself from the memory, and (4) closure, in which the activity is brought to a conclusion.

Polkinghorne, D. E. 1988). *Narrative Knowing and the Human Sciences.* Albany: State University of New York.

The term narrative, particularly as a form of expression, is analyzed in this book. The role of the narrative in history, literature, psychology, and in human existence is reviewed.

Sarbin, T. R. (1986). *Narrative Psychology: The Storied Nature of Human Conduct.* New York: Praeger.

This scholarly book presents an excellent background on the central role played by stories and storytelling in our everyday lives.

Shank, R. C. (1985). The quest to understand thinking. *Byte,* 10, 143-155.

Shank notes, "Knowledge is a collection of stories. We interpret reality through our stories and open up our realities to others when we tell our stories."

Shank, R. (1990). *Tell Me A Sory: A New Look at Real and Artificial Memory.* New York: Scribner.

This leading cognitive scientist explains that finding and listening to stories is a key part of thinking about life. "Thinking depends very much on storytelling and story understanding, and that is the subject of this book. Knowledge is stories!"

SOCIAL NETWORKS AND SOCIAL SUPPORT

REMINISCING IS A POWERFUL TOOL that helps people build their social networks of friends, thereby helping people receive the social support that is vital to health and well-being. These resources provide background on the nature of social networks and social support.

Barrera, M., & Ainlay, S. (1983). The structure of social support: A conceptual and empirical analysis. *American Journal of Community Psychology*, 11, 133-157.

This article provides theory and research on the importance of social support.

Benum, K., Dalgard, O. S., & Sørensen, T. (1987). Social network stimulation: Health promotion in a high-risk group of middle-aged women. *Acta Psychiatrica Scandinavica Supplement,* 337(76), 33-41.

This research article describes a successful intervention to increase social support among people.

Beverfelt, E. (1990). The public authorities' contributions to families caring for elderly people. *Gerontological Article Number 10-90.* Oslo, Norway: Norwegian Gerontological Institute.

The article makes a case for government's providing flexible, reliable, and continuing support systems for families that want to help their elder members remain in their own homes as long as the elders wish and as long as is possible.

Gottlieb, B. (1981). *Social Networks and Social Support.* Beverly Hills, CA: Sage.

The importance of social support for health and well-being is presented in this classic resource.

Gottlieb, B. (Ed.). (1987). Using social support to protect and promote health. *Journal of Primary Prevention,* 8, 49-70.

This article describes some ways in which social support can help promote and protect well-being.

Knipscheer, K. (1991, September). *Aging, Social Environment and Social Support.* Paper presented at the Second European Congress of Gerontology, Madrid, Spain.

This article is one of the best in relating healthy aging to social support from a healthy social environment.

Maton, K. (1987). Patterns and psychological correlates of material support: The bi-directionality hypothesis. *American Journal of Community Psychology,* 15, 185-207.

Reciprocity in support, a two-way street in which both parties give and receive support, is described as important for healthy relationships.

Newman, D., Griffin, P., & Cole, M. (1989). *The Construction Zone.* Cambridge: Cambridge University.

This book develops ideas first presented by the Russian psychologist Vygotsky. His concept of the social elaboration of learning states that a person's development is influenced in significant ways by the mutual process of sharing information, knowledge, and experience.

Resnick, L. B., Levine, J. M., & Teasley, S. D. (Eds.) (1991). *Perspectives on Socially Shared Cognition.* Washington, DC: American Psychological Association.

This comprehensive book develops thoroughly the idea that our thoughts are not bound by our own person. We are influenced mutually by what we think and by how and when we communicate those thoughts.

Revenson, T. (1988). Epilogue: The social constructions of aging revisited. *The Community Psychologist, 22,* 13-14.

This article delves into what we think it means to be an older person and how we influence the thoughts of one another on that topic.

Roberts, B., and Thorsheim, H. (1991). Reciprocal ministry: A transforming vision of help and leadership. In R. E. Hess, K. I. Maton, and K. I. Pargament (Eds.), *Religion and Prevention in Mental Health: Community Intervention,* (pp. 51-67). New York: Haworth.

The article shows how social support decreases over the life-span, both from friends and family members, and describes a data-based factor named "Investment in Community" as a remedy which increases social support.

Roberts, B., & Thorsheim, H. (1986). A partnership approach to consultation: The process and results of a major primary prevention field experiment. In J. G. Kelly & R. E. Hess (Eds.), *Prevention in Human Services,* 4(3/4) (pp.151-186). New York: Haworth.

This study identifies the keys for health and well-being: developing social support and mutual empowerment, in the form of knowing others' names; being asked to become involved; caring for others; and having skills for linking up with others.

Sauer, W. J., & Coward, R. C. (Eds.). (1985). *Social Support Networks and the Care of the Elderly.* New York: Springer.

This article presents additional information about the central role of social support and social support networks on the health and well-being of elders.

Thorsheim, H., & Roberts, B. (1995). Reminiscing and telling one's story: Finding common ground and mutual social support. In B. Haight & J. Webster (Eds.), *The Art and Science of Reminiscing: Theory, Research, Methods and Applications* (pp. 193-204). London: Taylor and Francis.

The chapter describes some possibilities for practitioners and researchers who are interested in designing reminiscing activities that encourage social support. The chapter was the forerunner to this book.

SPECIAL QUALITIES OF ELDERS' STORIES

ELDERS ARE JUST AS UNIQUE as people of any age group. These resources detail some of the ways in which elders are unique.

Adams, C., Labouvie-Vief, G., Hobart, C. J., & Dorosz, M. (1990). Adult age differences in story recall style. *Journal of Gerontology, 45(1)*, 12-27.

A point to be taken from this article is that younger and older adults may differ in their styles of remembering a story. The authors found that older adults were more likely to transform the story into a moral or lesson to be learned, whereas younger adults tended to preserve a story by paraphrasing it.

Adelman, M. B., & Bankoff, E. (1990). Life-span concerns: Implications for mid-life adult singles. In H. Giles, N. Coupland, & J. Wiemann (Eds.), *Fulbright Colloquium Series: No. 8. Communication, Health and the Elderly* (pp. 64-91). Manchester, England: University of Manchester.

This article explains how the issues people focus on are different at different stages of life. These questions may influence the kind of story they tell.

Langer, E., Chanowitz, B., Palmerino, M., Jacobs, S., Rhodes, M., & Thayer, P. (1990). Nonsequential development and aging. In C. N. Alexander & E. J. Langer (Eds.), *Higher Stages of Human Development* (pp. 114-136). New York: Oxford University.

The chapter points out that certain psychological interventions can alter what might otherwise be considered irreversible signs of aging.

Maitland, D. (1991). *Aging as Counterculture: A Vocation for the Later Years*. New York: Pilgrim.

Maitland reflects on how perceptions change in special ways as one moves from the morning, to the afternoon, and into the evening of life.

Nelson, E. A. (1992). Aged heterogeneity: Fact or fiction? *Gerontologist,* 32(1), 17-23.

This research article shows that, contrary to what some would believe, individual differences increase, rather than decrease, as people age.

Schaie, K. W. (1983). The Seattle longitudinal study: A 21-year investigation of psychometric intelligence. In K. W. Schaie (Ed.), *Longitudinal Studies of Adult Psychological Development.* New York: Guilford.

This research describes how the developmental process continues in adulthood.

Seim, S. (1989). Teenagers become adult and elderly. *Norwegian Gerontological Institute Report* 5-1989. Oslo, Norway.

This remarkable study, conducted in Norway and printed in English, is a unique study of the same group of persons from the time they were teenagers until they were elderly people. It focuses on intelligence and personality. The report highlights the fact that, given the usual process of aging, negative changes do not occur until very old age.

WRITING LIFE STORIES

IF YOU ARE INTERESTED IN WRITTEN LIFE STORIES and memoirs, you will enjoy the following resources. This list was compiled by reminiscing facilitator Fins Peterson, who has conducted numerous workshops on helping people write their stories.

Evans, F.-M. (1984). *Changing Memories into Memoirs: A Guide to Writing your Life Story.* New York: Barnes and Noble.

A chatty guide, filled with the techniques of writing.

Goldberg, N. (1986). *Writing Down the Bones: Freeing the Writer Within.* Boston: Shambala.

Judith Guest says this guide "gives people permission to think the thoughts that come, to write them down and make sense of them in any way they wish."

Gulsvig, M. (1987). *First Writes: Forty Writing Exercises for Older Adults.* Madison, WI: BiFolkal Productions.

A loose-leaf notebook uses the slotting method to motivate hesitant writers. Filling in the blanks leads to writing a memory story.

Kanin, R. (1986). *Write the Story of Your Life.* Baltimore: Genealogical Publications.

This book provides techniques to give you the confidence needed to put the story of your life into book form.

Lyons, R. (1984). *Autobiography: A Reader for Writers.* New York: Oxford University.

The author prefaces brief memoirs by forty-six famous people with insightful suggestions for relating these memories to one's own writings. The book offers valuable information about how people write.

~ *Appendices* ~

The activity aids outlined in the following appendices may be duplicated or you may use them as guides for creating your own.

~ *Appendix I* ~

1A. NAME TAGS

Bring-a-Thing Party	**Bring-a-Thing Party**
Bring-a-Thing Party	**Bring-a-Thing Party**
Bring-a-Thing Party	**Bring-a-Thing Party**

1 B. BRING-A-THING PERSONAL STORY RECORD

This is your personal story record to take home with you:

Your Name _____

What is the Bring-a-Thing item you will be talking about?

_____

_____

Jot down a few words about your *thing*. Others will remember you and your story better if you give plenty of details about the item you brought.

- Who does it remind you of?

_____

_____

- What happened?

_____

_____

- Where were you?

_____

_____

- When?

_____

_____

- Why is this thing important to you?

_____

_____

1 b. Bring-a-Thing
Personal Story Record *(continued)*

Jot down a title you might give to your story.

_____

Name of your partner

_____

What is the Bring-a-Thing your partner talked about?

_____

Write down the title of your partner's story.

_____

Group Sharing

In the group sharing part of the Bring-a-Thing activity, others will tell about their Bring-a-Thing. If you wish, you may use the space below to list names of other people who talked. Describe their Bring-a-Things to help you remember them.

_____
Person's Name   Their Bring-a-Thing

_____
Person's Name   Their Bring-a-Thing

_____
Person's Name   Their Bring-a-Thing

_____
Person's Name   Their Bring-a-Thing

_____
Person's Name   Their Bring-a-Thing

_____
Person's Name   Their Bring-a-Thing

_____
Person's Name   Their Bring-a-Thing

1c. Activity Evaluation Form A

Please share any thoughts you have about any of the following:

1. What do you consider to have been today's most valuable experience?

_____

Why?

_____

_____

_____

2. What aspects of the activity could have been improved? How?

_____

_____

_____

3. Any additional comments?

_____

_____

_____

_____

_____

_____

1D. ACTIVITY EVALUATION FORM B

Here is an alternative evaluation form created by the Rev. Omar Otterness, founder of the Cooperative Older Adult Ministry. The C.O.A.M. is a coalition of twenty-six congregations in Minneapolis, Minnesota.

1. What happened in this activity? _____

2. What did you do together, in *your* eyes? _____

_____

3. What worked to encourage what happened? _____

_____

4. How did you feel about what happened? _____

_____

5. What did you get out of this? _____

_____

6. In what way(s) was this helpful to you (e.g., a learning experience)? _____

_____

7. What do you think your partner got out of this? _____

_____

8. Can you think of other settings or structures where this could be done as well (or better)? _____

_____

9. How did you come to participate? Check those that apply:

_____ Invitations   _____ Announcement

_____ Church Bulletin   _____ Arm-Twisting

_____ Volunteer   _____ Other _____

10. Would you do this again? _____

11. Would you recommend this to your friends? _____

~ *Appendix II* ~
Overhead Masters for Reminiscing Activities

The following pages are masters
for overhead transparencies
that illustrate the steps involved
in the Bring-a-Thing activities.

Step 1

FIND A PARTNER

Step 2

JOT
DOWN

Step 3

NAME YOUR STORY

Step 4

TELLER   LISTENER

Step 5

LISTENER
REPEATS BACK

Step 6

SWITCH ROLES

~ *Appendix III* ~

Resources for
Reminiscing Activities

American Association for State and Local History
    530 Church Street   www.aaslh.org
    Suite 600
    Nashville TN 37219   e-mail: history@aaslh.org
    615-255-2971

To find your own state's historical society, contact the American Association for State and Local History. Your state historical society can put you in contact with your local Oral History Association.

Area Agency on Aging

These agencies were established by the Older Americans Act. In Minnesota, for example, there are fourteen geographical Area Agencies on Aging. This large statewide network puts people in contact with services and publications such as book reviews, advertisements, and information of interest to elders.

Bi-Folkal Productions
    809 Williamson Street
    Madison WI 53703
    608-251-2818

This service has a free catalog that advertises books, objects, and ideas that encourage the sharing of life experiences.

Elder Books
>PO Box 490
>Forest Knolls CA 94933
>1 800-909-2673

>Elder Books has books and activity resources to facilitate reminiscence.

Black Storytellers Organization
>Mary Carter Smith
>P.O. Box 11484
>Baltimore MD 21239
>410-323-4458

>Mary Carter Smith, co-founder of this organization, has told us she would be pleased to hear from you. Good books recommended by Mary Carter Smith include Homespun by Jimmie Neal Smith, the founder of the National Storytelling Association, and the anthology of African American folktales Talk That Talk, edited by Linda Goss and Marian Barnes.

Elderhostel
>Elderhostel Registration Associates   www.elderhostel.org
>75 Federal Street
>Boston MA 02110
>617-426-8056

>At the organization's website, you may type in a term like reminiscing to find out where courses on those topics are being taught and to learn details about the course.

Generations
>American Society on Aging
>833 Market Street
>Room 516
>San Francisco CA 94103
>415-543-2617

>Generations is published quarterly. Contact the American Society on Aging for current subscription prices.

National Storytelling Association
    116 West Main Street
    Jonesborough TN 37659
    423-753-2171 or 1-800-525-4514

The National Storytelling Association publishes an annual catalog
that is available at no cost.

National Oral History Association
    P.O. Box 97234
    Baylor University
    Waco TX 76798-7234
    817-755-2764

Or, for an example of a state affiliate, contact
    Oral History Association of Minnesota
    Oral History Office
    Minnesota History Center
    345 Kellogg Blvd. West
    St. Paul MN 55107
    612-296-6980, ask for the Oral History Office

Minnesota's unique program has developed a workshop package
that includes pamphlets. The workshops on oral history are presented for civic organizations, community groups and churches.
The association would be pleased to share information about their
program.

Senior Citizens News and Views

Senior citizen centers have established networks in most states
and publish newsletters with titles such as Senior Citizens News
and Views.

Southern Order of Storytellers
    c/o Pat Wilson, Treasurer
    Georgia Advocacy Office
    315 West Ponce de Leon Avenue
    Decatur GA 30030

~ *Other Titles from Elder Books* ~

Reminiscence: Uncovering A Lifetime of Memories
by Carmel Sheridan
Reminiscing is a healing activity for people with Alzheimer's disease. This book explains the simple techniques involved in stimulating memories. It outlines themes to explore as well as hundreds of meaningful activities involving reminiscence.   **$14.95**

Activity Ideas for the Budget-Minded by Debra Cassistre
This popular treasury of tried and true activity ideas is now back by popular demand in a revised and expanded edition. Already used by thousands of activity directors, this new edition is packed with dozens of hands-on, ready-to-use, budget stretching activities. These low-cost activity ideas will give your program an inexpensive boost, create variety and give residents the kind of stimulation and entertainment they deserve.   **$10.95**

Failure-Free Activities for the Alzheimer's Patient by Carmel Sheridan
This award-winning book describes dozens of simple, non-threatening activities which are suitable for persons with Alzheimer's disease. The author describes how to focus on the abilities that remain rather than the patient's deficits, and shows how to create activities which capitalize on existing strengths.   **$10.95**

Tell Me A Story
This is a set of 56 idea cards designed specifically to encourage communication through reminiscence, storytelling and some role play.
A simple reminiscence tool, *Tell Me A Story* can be used by visitors as well as family and professional caregivers who find it difficult to initiate conversation with frail, older adults. Set in large type, these cards are sturdy for long-lasting use.   **$14.95**

So Much More than A Sing-A-Long by Neta Wenrick, MS, RMT-BC
This tremendous resource book is bursting with dozens of therapeutic activities for older adults. Music therapist Neta Wenrick presents original, interesting topics which are excellent for use with large and small groups. A must "one-stop" resource book for activity directors and music therapists.   **$16.95**

Order Form

PLEASE SEND ME:

QTY:	TITLE	PRICE/COPY	TOTALS
____	I Remember When	$16.95	_____
____	Reminiscence	$14.95	_____
____	Activity Ideas for the Budget Minded	$10.95	_____
____	Failure-Free Actitities for the Alzheimer's Patient	$10.95	_____
____	Tell Me A Story	$14.95	_____
____	So Much More than A Sing-A-Long	$16.95	_____

TOTAL FOR BOOKS . . . . _____
TOTAL SALES TAX . . . . _____
TOTAL SHIPPING . . . . _____
AMOUNT ENCLOSED . . . . _____

Shipping: $2.95 for first book, $1.75 for each additional book;
California residents, please add 8.25% sales tax.

Name _____

Address _____

City _____ State ___ Zip ___

SEND TO:

Elder Books   P.O. Box 490   Forest Knolls CA 94933
Tel: 1800 909 COPE (2673)   FAX: 415 488 4720
Email: info@ElderBooks.com
www.ElderBooks.com